ADVAN
CHILD CARE
BUSINESS
STRATEGIES

Secrets to Profitability, Expansion, and Wealth Creation

Brian & Carol Duprey

Published by: **Child Care Genius LLC**
P.O. Box 73
Stillwater, ME 04489
www.ChildCareGenius.com

info@ChildCareGenius.com

First edition 2022
Printed in the United States of America

About the Authors

Brian and Carol Duprey are two of the world's leading experts in child care profitability, expansion, wealth creation, and mindset. Together, they have operated ten child care centers in the last 25 years.

Brian is an eight-year U.S. Navy veteran, and Carol is a ten-year U.S. Navy veteran. They met as instructors teaching anti-submarine warfare tactics in the early 1990s in Virginia Beach.

After dating, Brian and Carol married, left the military, and moved to Maine to start a new life. Carol started a job as a bookkeeper for a child care center, and Brian started his own advertising agency.

Eventually, Carol bought the center and began a nearly 30-year career in the child care business. Brian joined Carol and helped run the school full-time after about 3 years, embarking on an ambitious expansion plan.

In 2017, Brian became one of the very first certified coaches in the child care industry. Carol got certified in 2018.

Since 2017, Brian and Carol have coached tens of thousands of child care owners worldwide to increased profitability through their books, courses, trainings, coaching, and podcast.

In 2018, Brian wrote a book that has been the number one best-selling child care business book of all time. Brian no longer believes in many of the nuggets he wrote in that book, hence the release of the book you are holding in your hands, which is a much better book on child care profitability.

Brian co-authored a second book called ***The Child Care Happiness Guide: Secrets to Living Your Best Life in and Out of the Classroom***. This book quickly became an Amazon #1 New Release Best Seller and is an amazing book that all child care teachers, directors, and owners should read.

In November 2020, Brian left his job and spent the entire year of 2021 working alongside Carol to build their real estate dynasty into a multi-million dollar business.

In 2021, Brian and Carol also began collaborating on a book together, and in early 2022, ***The Art of the Tour: Tips, Tools, and Tactics to Increase Tours and Conversions at Your Child Care Center*** was published. It quickly became an Amazon #1 New Release Best Seller. It is the best book on the market on how to do a child care tour and follow up appropriately.

In 2022, Brian and Carol launched the ***Child Care Genius Podcast***™. Each week they discuss topics dedicated to helping the listener become a seven-figure child care owner. It is one of the fastest-growing podcasts on the internet today.

Also in 2022, Brian and Carol published two mindset books: ***Child Care Mindset: 30 Days of Growth and Transformation*** and ***Child Care Mindset: Dreams, Goals, and Gratitude Journal***. These resources are valuable for all team members at a child care center to improve mindsets and work together with a common purpose.

All books are available at ChildCareGenius.com/Books.

Brian and Carol live in their amazing lakefront dream home on Pushaw Lake in Glenburn, Maine, and enjoy boating, jet-skiing, kayaking, and snowmobiling.

Thank you for reading! Please visit our website at ChildCareGenius.com to see a list of services we provide. Please drop us a line and let us know how this book or the others we have written have impacted you. We return all emails, and you can reach us via email at info@ChildCareGenius.com.

Table of Contents

Chapter 4: Dynasty Culture   72

Chapter 5: Advanced HR and Legal   89

Chapter 6: Dynasty Financial Strategies   96

Chapter 7: Dynasty Marketing Strategy   117

Foreword

I cannot adequately express how honored I was when Brian and Carol approached me about writing the foreword to this book. Brian is a former colleague of mine, and I consider both Brian and Carol to be the world's leading authorities on child care expansion and profitability. When asked, I was quick to say yes, as I was thrilled to have a way to give something back to this amazing couple. You see, they are the type of people who would do anything to jump in and help someone in need. They'd not only give you the shirt off their backs, but they'd also help you figure out why you didn't have a shirt and set you up with a plan to obtain all the shirts you need in the future. Then they'd check in to see how it was going and if you were hitting your "shirt" goals.

My cheesy analogy aside, if you haven't had the pleasure of meeting them yet, just know that Brian and Carol Duprey are the real deal. They are kind-hearted, generous, inspiring people and they are motivated by helping as many people as they can - especially child care business owners.

Brian and Carol have owned ten child care centers over the years, and they have lived through every situation you could possibly imagine. Their experiences are invaluable when it comes to providing coaching and mentorship. Not only do they know firsthand how important child care and preschool programs are for children and families, but they truly have a heart for it. They LOVE child care and the impact they get to make on the world through this business. They love it so much that they want to help as many other providers as possible build successful businesses so more children are impacted.

That's why if you are a child care business owner, or are considering becoming one, you need to read any book they put out. This book, ***Advanced Child Care Business Strategies: Secrets to Profitability, Expansion, and Wealth Creation***, is their best one yet. And I have read every single book they've written, so I feel I can say that with authority. This book goes deeper into many business building strategies and offers more ideas than any other child care business book on the market today.

The intention of this book is to help the child care business owner that wants to grow and expand to create their own child care dynasty. It is for the business owner that wants to build a legacy and create true wealth. This book contains many advanced strategies to that point, but even a beginner will get a ton out of these pages.

I've personally been in the child care industry for about 25 years. Most of those years I spent in home daycare, but I did own my own child care center licensed for 120 children for 5 years. I was one of those people that had a passion for the business, but little business training. I made so many mistakes along the way, and I wish this book would have been available to me back then! I think it would have given me a shortcut to success. In my case, the chapters and "Secrets" about financial strategies, expansion strategies, and financing options would have been most helpful. But this book has it all: goal setting, mindset, corporate structure, corporate leadership, HR, legal, marketing, exit strategy, and more! If it's important to successful business growth, it's in the book.

I hope you enjoy reading it as much as I did, and I hope it helps you to make your child care dreams come true.

Sindye Alexander
Child Care Business, Marketing, & Culture Expert
Author, Trainer, Speaker

Sindye Alexander has over 25 years of experience in the child care field as a home provider, center owner, marketer, trainer, speaker, course creator, and author. While building her child care business she fell in love with marketing. She currently provides digital and content marketing services for private clients with businesses related to the child care industry. Sindye has a particular passion for inspiring child care leaders to create a positive workplace culture which will impact the industry by reducing staff turnover rates and by contributing to increased program quality. Her book: **Relationship Roadmap: Real-World Strategies for Building a Positive, Collaborative Culture in Your Preschool** *is dedicated to providing owners and directors actionable tips and tactics for doing just that. She loves helping other child care business owners and directors grow and succeed through training and speaking at live and virtual events. Sindye resides in northern Michigan with her husband, Chad. They have four grown children and three grandchildren. Sindye values time with her family and enjoys traveling – especially camping and cruising!*

Acknowledgments

To our amazing parents, Roger and Susan Duprey and Dave and Ella Stotler, thank you for teaching us the value of hard work and the importance of family.

To our amazing children, thank you for being such a blessing to raise.

Thank you to our daughter, Aubrey Knorr, for proofreading and editing this book.

A very special thank you to one of the best certified child care coaches we know, Sindye Alexander. Thank you for taking the time to write the foreword to this book and for the fantastic contribution you have made to the child care industry.

To all of the exceptional child care owners who have allowed us to guide them through our books, training, podcast, and coaching over the years, thank you for believing in us, as we surely believe in you!

To our Lord and Savior Jesus Christ, thank you for blessing us with the talents of writing, speaking, and coaching, and we look forward to someday being told: "Well done, thou good and faithful servant."

Dedication

To our brothers and sisters in uniform who risk their lives each and every day, thank you for making it possible for us to be entrepreneurs and live out our dreams in freedom.

Your service and sacrifice are always on our minds and will never be forgotten.

Introduction

You are holding the most advanced child care business strategy book in the world. In this book, we teach you how to build a child care dynasty.

What is a child care dynasty? It is owning multiple child care centers that produce significant income that can pay dividends for generations. Your dynasty may have three centers; it may have 100.

If you follow the secrets in this book, you will make millions in the child care business. How do we know it can be done? We have done it, and we have coached many clients to seven-figure profits.

This book will not teach you how to deal with a child with behavioral issues; there are plenty of books for that.

This book will not teach you how to deal with problem employees; you can find a book for that.

This book is all about the side of the business no one wants to talk about....PROFIT. Without profit, your teachers cannot be paid. Without profit, the rent does not get paid. Without profit, you are out of business very quickly.

If you treat your employees, vendors, charities, and the planet right, then stop worrying and go out and make as much moolah as you want. The IRS will thank you for it! (Don't worry, we will give you some good tax strategies to help you there too!)

Dream big and put in the work. Your great-great-grandchildren will thank you for it.

Preface

Let us be the first to admit that we are not professional writers. You may notice grammatical errors in this book; it is self-published. We are child care center dynasty builders who have made millions in the child care business and in the real estate business, and we want to share our knowledge with you. Judge us more by our intent and the content herein than by the delivery.

We recommend that you take notes in the book. We have included a notes section at the end of each chapter, and there are places to take notes in several parts of the book. Please do so, as it will help you remember them.

We have included several book recommendations throughout the book, each placed in the Secret where they are most applicable. If you are struggling or need extra help with that Secret, we recommend reading the recommended book to help you. When you read these books, we recommend revisiting these Secrets afterward to help give them more context and meaning; you will get much more out of the book by doing so.

You may criticize us for not offering you more content on each Secret, as some people want to shortcut the path to success and want everything done for them. We want you to take the ideas we give and make them your own, bring them to life, and make them better than we did. By doing it for you, we would be limiting you, and that is not what we are about. We want everyone reading this book to be more successful than we are.

We also promote our favorite products in this book, "OURS!" We do not apologize for that. We have the most advanced product line of tools and coaching to help grow your child care business; why wouldn't we brag about it and encourage you to move your business forward?

Thank you for all you do to make a difference in the world. We are excited to be a small part of your success story. Now go forth and build your child care dynasty; we will be your biggest cheerleaders. If you would like us to coach you to greatness, be sure to check out Child Care Genius University, our amazing coaching, and mentorship program.

Chapter 1

Success Goals and Mindset

"My goal is to build a life I don't need a vacation from."
~ Rob Hill

In this chapter, we will set goals for your business and get you in the proper mindset for building your child care dynasty. We can promise you that you will never wake up one day with a child care dynasty and wonder how you got there. Expansion is intentional and will kick your butt if you let it. Most center owners (about 95%) will never attempt to open a second center. Do you have what it takes to be in the top 5%?

In building a child care dynasty, an owner will experience many ups and downs, highs and lows, and will want to quit many times. We have been there too many times to count. When you are the closest to victory, you will want to quit the most. Be steadfast in your resolve, and be richly rewarded.

Mindset is something that we have been coaching and teaching for many years. You cannot create a dynasty without the proper mindset. In this chapter, we will help you to get your mindset right, set audacious goals, and prepare mentally for the challenge of creating a legacy for your family. Your decisions will affect your family for generations; we are proud that you have trusted us to guide you, and we will do our best to steer you in the right direction.

Do not skip over this chapter because you want to fast forward to the technical aspects of becoming a seven-figure child care owner. For some of you, this chapter will be painful. For some, it may seem boring or unrelated to success, but we can promise you that if you master the areas of Chapter 1, you will succeed in business and in life beyond your wildest dreams.

We firmly believe that you can do everything right and still fail if you do not have the proper mindset for success. This book is a great start to helping you get that proper mindset.

Secret #1

The End is the Beginning

Imagine running a race where you had no idea where the end of the race was. It could be a mile or 100 miles. You would have no idea; would you ever dare to enter it? How would you train for such a race? If you did start training and it started getting tough, would you stick with it?

The end is the beginning.

We want you to start thinking about the end. The end gives you a goal, something to strive for. The end keeps you from quitting when the going gets tough; what does your end look like? In most cases, the end is the last day you own your schools, either by selling or having a family member take over operations.

We have met many child care owners who have had their single small center for 30+ years and, after selling, do not have much to live on. They worked hard for a long time; they didn't make smart financial choices along the way. Not because they weren't smart but because no one showed them what the end would look like 30 years ago, so they never had a goal to work towards. For them, the race had no finish line.

If we had sat down with this person 30 years ago and asked them what they wanted the end to look like, more than likely, it would be vastly different than where they ended up. Why? Because life gets in the way.

Life has a way of passing you by if you let it, and the busier you are, the faster it seems to go. This person was comfortable, both from job satisfaction and a financial standpoint. They made enough money, and they made a difference. They were content. If 30 years ago that is all they wanted, then we would be the first to say, "Congratulations; well done." In our experience, most owners regret making poor choices along the way, and when they are ready to exit the business, they are not very happy with the end result.

We want to change your future. We want to change your legacy. Your grandchildren's-grandchildren could benefit financially from your decisions in the next few years. Make them wisely, and you will know generational wealth, which you can use however you wish to leave your mark on the world. In our case, we have educational and entrepreneurial trust funds to take care of several generations of our family. We can help you get there too.

Let's do the following exercise in pencil, do not use a pen. When you are done with the book and have learned all that we are going to teach you, you will want to come back to this Secret and look at your goals again, and very likely, they will have changed. At that point, you can write them in pen and then hang them on the wall in your office.

Now get a pencil, and we will wait for you—no cheating by skipping this section. If you are serious about building a child care dynasty, you need to do everything we lay out in the book without leaving anything out. Now let's get you in the proper frame of mind. It's time to change your life!

Let's start by thinking about the end; what year will that be?
Year: _____

How many locations would you like to own at that point?
Locations: _____

What will the value of your real estate portfolio be at that point?
Real Estate Value: $_____

What would you like your net worth to be at that point?
Net Worth: $_____

I plan on owning other businesses or investment real estate.
Value: $_____

Other: _____
Value: $_____

This exercise may be hard for you at this point in time; we understand that.

The secret is to put them down on paper; you can always refine them later.

Remember this important Secret on Success Goals and Mindset: ***The end is the beginning.***

Secret #2

Think Like a Multi-Millionaire

Now that we have our end goal, let's prepare to win mentally. The problem with writing down ambitious goals is that you never will take action if you don't believe you can achieve them.

You will <u>NEVER</u> outgrow your self-image. You will never earn more money than you think you are worth. You will never be a positive influence if your head is filled with negative thoughts.

If you only have one center, you will likely have a single-center mindset. Whatever income you make is what you feel deep down you are worth. To build a child care dynasty, you need to start thinking and acting like a multi-millionaire. This will require quite a bit of work, but if you want the goals you wrote in Secret #1, you must be willing to do whatever it takes.

We all have a past. We cannot escape from it; it is always in our minds. For some of us, those memories dominate our thoughts on a daily or even continuous basis. Many of you have had unthinkable things happen to you in the past. Those things helped to mold you into the person you are today.

The gray matter that occupies the six inches between our ears has the power to give us immense pleasure, or incredible pain, all with just a single thought. This God-given miracle, which we call our brain, is more powerful than any computer in the world, and you own it! You get to use it however you wish, and if you use it correctly, it can be a source of joy like you have never seen before. You can also use it to be miserable for the rest of your life. It is your choice. When you sit in front of your laptop, you can choose which program to open, and the computer does what you tell it to do. Same with your brain, you have a choice of which file to open, and if you accidentally open the wrong file, you need to close it immediately.

Stop living in the past. It is time to move on from whatever is holding you back. When water flows over a dam, it never will return to the same spot and do it again; it moves on, and so must you. Learning from the past is imperative; being held hostage by it will block your present and future success.

Book Recommendation:
When Your Past Is Hurting Your Present: Getting Beyond Fears That Hold You Back
by Sue Augustine

Each day we wake up, we choose where to spend time in our minds. Focusing on the present will keep you focused on your goals and keep you from being shackled to the memories that will drag you down.

Looking back in history, you will find very successful people who have had horrible things happen to them. They found a way to put the past behind them and live in the present.

Some of you may self-medicate with drugs and alcohol to drown out past negative feelings. It may work temporarily, but it will almost always make things worse in the long run because this new issue now quickly becomes the issue you have guilt over, and the cycle continues.

We highly recommend getting professional help if you have thoughts of suicide or you simply can't get over the past on your own. There is nothing wrong with asking for help. Once we get our brain focused on the present, we can unleash the power of our brain and help us accomplish our goals and dreams.

One of the best ways to combat negative thoughts is with positive ones. Positive thoughts and negative thoughts cannot coexist. So when you have dominant negativity in your mind, it is time to dump positivity in your brain. Positive podcasts and books are the best way to force-feed yourself happy thoughts. Finding something positive will help to release dopamine (the pleasure chemical) in your brain. You will feel better and get past the negative thoughts.

If life were fair, it would be boring. We would all have the same car, house, clothes, toys, etc. The truth is we don't want it to be fair; we want to know that if we work hard, we will be rewarded for our efforts. Some people will work harder than you and not attain your success. Some people won't work as hard and may become more successful. Our job is to focus on the person who stares back in the mirror and doesn't worry about anyone else's success.

Envy of others is the reason you may think things are unfair. Jealousy is a dangerous thing. It causes us to lose sight of our goals and become fixated on others. Go find what you want in life and forget about everyone else.

You are the master of your fate. Stop blaming others for where you are in life; you are not a victim but a winner. We believe in you and are confident that you will accomplish your goals and dreams, and we are here to help you get there.

Each day your brain receives tens of thousands of images, most of which are stored as negative thoughts in your brain. A person today will receive more negative images in their brain in one day than someone who lived 100 years ago would receive in their lifetime. No wonder negative thoughts dominate our minds.

Looking in the mirror is a negative image for many people. Many people hate what they look like. Hollywood has painted a picture in our minds of what beauty looks like, and many of us have fallen for it, and when we see ourselves, it makes us unhappy.

You are beautiful! You are amazing! You are special! You are unique! There is only one of you, and the mold was broken when you were born. It is time to start eliminating negative thoughts about yourself and start creating new, positive ones. You will never outgrow your perception of yourself. If you think you are a failure, you will be. If you think like a success, you already are.

Book Recommendation:
The Happiness Advantage
by Shawn Achor

The best way to drown out negative thoughts is by putting more positivity in your brain. Reading positive mental attitude (PMA) books is one of the best ways, and we recommend reading this for 15-30 minutes a day in this type of book. Doing so will help build your self-image and help you to counter those negative thoughts. We believe in you, and soon you will believe in yourself.

Remember this important Secret on Success Goals and Mindset: *Think like a multi-millionaire.*

Secret #3

Define Your "Why"

Why do you want to become a millionaire or a multi-millionaire? Why are you in the child care business in the first place? Have you ever sat down and asked yourself why you do what you do? Well, we are going to do that now.

I am in the child care business because:

_____

_____

_____

_____

_____

_____

_____

_____

Why do I want to become a multi-millionaire?

_____

_____

_____

_____

_____

_____

_____

Now that we know why we do what we do each day, we can define a plan. It all starts with the why. When things get tough, and they will, you can revisit your why, giving you the motivation to go on. Without a why; quitting will always be an option. When your why is defined and becomes a motivator, you will stop at nothing to achieve it.

Remember this important Secret on Success Goals and Mindset: *Define your "why."*

Secret #4

Have a Gratitude Mindset

What are you thankful for? You have this amazing life you have created for yourself; to whom are you grateful for helping you get to this point? No one becomes successful alone; normally, hundreds or thousands of people, all play a small or a large part of your success.

It is time to give thanks. It is time to make this a daily thought; it will help you to lead a happier, more fulfilling life. We recommend getting a gratitude journal and writing in it every day. What are you thankful for? Who are you thankful for? Let's take a few moments and write down 10 things that you are grateful for:

1. _Georgia_ Grateful for my
2. _Mom & Dad_ ability to cope!
3. _my home_
4. _my car_ my drive to do
5. _my job_ the best.
6. _my career_ Sex!
7. _my work ethic_ kissing —
8. _my ability to create/make_
9. _my friends_
10. _my extended family_

Get a gratitude journal and write at least one thing you are thankful for each and every day; early in the morning will be the best time. Beginning your day with grateful thoughts will kickstart your brain with positivity, and you will have a much happier and more productive day.

When something bad happens in your life or negative thoughts start creeping into your brain, pull out your gratitude journal and start reading (and writing.) Your mindset will quickly become more joyful as you focus on things that bring joy to your life.

When you get to Secret #98, you will see there is a certain journal that we recommend (hint: it is one we created).

Remember this important Secret on Success Goals and Mindset: *Have a gratitude mindset.*

Secret #5

Be a Difference Maker

Each day, you can make a difference in hundreds of people's lives, many of whom you have never met or may never meet. What we do daily matters and affects much more than our little world.

There are the people you have a close personal relationship with: your spouse, kids, employees, friends, customers, and neighbors. These people know you well, and this is where you will make the most difference in the world.

Then there are those people with whom you interact daily that you do not know: the bank teller, cashier, police officer, mail carrier, taxi driver, drive-thru attendant, homeless person, customer service representative, etc.

Each day we interact with a lot of people, some of whom are hurting. You have the chance to make a positive impact on these people's lives. A kind word, a compliment, empathy, a big tip; whatever your way of impacting others positively, be sure to always choose to leave people better off than when they first interacted with you.

Compliments are a way of making a massive difference in someone's day. Since most of us think negatively about ourselves often, having someone compliment us on anything is usually very flattering and will more than likely make their day. Helping others feel better about themselves will make you feel better about yourself.

Send an email to someone you know telling them how much you appreciate them. Write a thank-you note to someone to express your feelings or appreciation. Buy a gift for someone who has made a difference in your life. Be a difference-maker.

Book Recommendation:
The Difference Maker
by Dr. John C. Maxwell

Your attitude and how you live your life is an example for others to follow and help to make a difference in their lives. When you become a multi-millionaire, and you do it with integrity, you will set an example for others to follow; you will make a difference in their individual lives.

Every Christmas Eve, our church does a candlelight service where all of the lights in the church are turned off, and a single candle is lit on stage. That candle, in turn, burns another candle without losing any of its flames. It sacrifices nothing to give light to another. That one candle eventually starts a chain reaction that lights the room full of candles; it all started with one.

You are that one. We are lighting your candle with this chapter on mindset. You are now the one that can go lift someone else up. You are the difference-maker. You can use your light to make others shine, and in return, if your light ever gets extinguished, just come back to this chapter, and we will light it again and again. We will always be here for you. We believe in you.

Remember this important Secret on Success Goals and Mindset: *Be a difference-maker.*

Secret #6

Listen to the Child Care Genius Podcast™

Each week, we record a podcast called the **Child Care Genius Podcast™.** We highly recommend that you go wherever you listen to podcasts and hit subscribe. We will also record the video and place it on YouTube, should you wish to see our faces and hear our voices.

We will teach mindset, profitability, employment, hiring, taxes, exit planning, diversification, and expansion. Please visit our website at ChildCareGenius.com to see a list of past episodes and to subscribe.

We will discuss topics to help you grow your child care business. Each episode is limited to 30 minutes, which for many of you equals your morning commute time. Just turn on our podcast and let us fill your mind with positive thoughts while you are on your way to work. If you want to watch the video of our podcast, visit our Child Care Genius YouTube Channel.

We hope you will take your valuable time and join us. We promise to teach you all of our Secrets and not hold anything back. If you like our podcast, please be so kind as to leave a review.

Remember this important Secret on Success Goals and Mindset: **Listen to the Child Care Genius Podcast™.**

Secret #7

Take a Tax-Deductible Vacation...Often!

Unplugging at regular intervals increases productivity when you return to the office by many folds. The more you rest, the harder you will work. You will get much more work done in 46 weeks by vacationing for 6 weeks than you will if you worked all 52 weeks, and you will be much happier and live longer because your stress level will be much lower.

We take a tax-deductible vacation each year and hold our annual corporate meeting retreat. We have an agenda, take minutes and set business goals for the year. We write off this yearly trip as a business expense.

Let's say you want to go to Las Vegas for a vacation. Reach out to child care centers in the Las Vegas area and do some tours (research) while you are there. Look at some commercial real estate while you are there. Keep good notes on what you do that is business-related, save business cards and keep receipts and you will be able to deduct most of the trip on your taxes.

How would you like to vacation with us? Later in the book (Secret #101) we will show you how to enjoy a tax-deductible vacation while lying on a beach with us and learning how to make millions in your child care business. How much fun will that be?

NOTE: *We are not accountants, be sure to contact your tax professional before taking any deduction.*

Remember this important Secret on Success Goals and Mindset: ***Take a tax-deductible vacation...often!***

Secret #8

Live a Healthy Lifestyle

It takes incredible stamina to build a multi-million-dollar business. We have done it twice (simultaneously), so we know that to be the case. In the early days, we would burn the candle at both ends (and even in the middle).

For the first 15 years of our businesses, we worked seven days a week, 48-50 weeks a year. We worked our butts off. We would do maintenance on the weekends, help out at the centers during the week, and in the evenings, we would work on paperwork and payroll. We did a lot wrong.

One thing we did right was we exercised and ate well during those early years. It gave us the stamina to endure those long days without collapsing or losing it mentally. We were both former military members, so we were used to exercising as part of our work routine.

Making a healthy lifestyle a priority is vital to long-term business success. In a previous Secret, we discussed vacationing often will cause you to get more work done than if you didn't go on vacation. Taking the time to exercise will yield more productivity in your day than if you did not do it. The biggest beneficiary to your health is you. You will get to live long enough to spend all the money we will help you create.

Eating healthy is at the forefront of a good health routine. If you are overweight, we recommend a calorie and food tracking app as a way to lose weight and keep it off. Calories burned needs to always be greater than calories consumed to lose weight.

Regarding exercise, we personally subscribe to Beachbody on Demand, where we have access to hundreds of exercise routines that we do together in the comfort of our own homes. Find an exercise program that works for you and do 30 minutes of exercise five times a week to stay healthy.

Find time to meditate as well. Sitting still and focusing on breathing will do wonders for stress reduction and increase your stamina and productivity. There are free apps you can download that will help you with this.

Living an unhealthy lifestyle will block you from reaping the rewards of your hard work. Your brain and body need rest, relaxation, and the proper mix of healthy fuel to work at maximum efficiency. Treat it well, and your brain and body will be with you for the long haul.

Drinking, smoking, caffeine, and drugs will take a toll on your body over time. Be very careful with these substances as they are success blockers. Moderation is the key.

Remember this important Secret on Success Goals and Mindset: *Live a healthy lifestyle.*

Secret #9

Enroll in a Mastermind Group

Book Recommendation:
Think and Grow Rich
by Napoleon Hill

One of our favorite books is ***Think and Grow Rich*** by Napoleon Hill. In this book, the author discusses the power of joining a mastermind group.

"Mastermind principle is the coordination of knowledge and effort of two or more people who work toward a definite purpose in the spirit of harmony." ~ Napoleon Hill

Having a group of child care center owners in a mastermind group with you is powerful. You can share ideas, share information, set goals, and talk about your dreams. You will get encouragement and support that you won't get anywhere else. The first mastermind I joined changed my life, and it was the relationships with the other owners that made it so powerful.

We are proud to operate two mastermind groups; we would love to have you join either one:

Child Care Genius Mastermind Private Facebook Group

This is a free mastermind that you will be in with other child care center owners. Some will be home daycare center owners; some will be multi-site owners. Everyone in the group is united in one mission, to become successful and profitable child care owners and leaders. To join, visit our website at: Facebook.com/groups/childcaregenius.

Child Care Genius University

This is a mastermind coaching and training university that will help your business grow in all areas. Visit ChildCareGenius.com/University for more information.

Remember this important Secret on Success Goals and Mindset: ***Enroll in a mastermind group.***

Secret #10

Get Out of Your Comfort Zone

Brian used to have a lot of fears; Carol is not afraid of anything. It made for an interesting dynamic when we went on vacation. Carol would go jump off a cliff; Brian would watch nervously from a safe distance. Carol would want to go skydiving and whitewater rafting, and Brian would kindly decline. Why would anyone want to jump out of a perfectly good airplane?

Then Brian started reading PMA (Positive Mental Attitude) books, which changed his life. He read a quote from Dr. John C. Maxwell: "Life begins at the end of your comfort zone." After reading this, Brian was a new person and has lived life to the fullest each day since.

Since then, Brian has been scuba diving, whitewater rafting (where he almost died after spending 20 mins in 40-degree water), skydiving, paragliding, and zip-lining worldwide. We both enjoy the adrenaline rush of living our lives just outside of our comfort zones. Does anyone want to zip-line with us on one of our *Child Care Genius Workations*? We will indeed be doing some amazing out-of-our-comfort-zone excursions!

What is holding you back from having an amazing life? Are you afraid of success? Do what is uncomfortable now to live a life of comfort later. Action cures fear, do what you are afraid of, and it will no longer have power over you.

YODO - You Only Die Once. This is our favorite saying. We say it all the time. Many people say YOLO as a way to justify risky behavior. The problem is we all die, but not everyone truly lives. We are all going to die, and we are all going to die exactly once. So go live your life as if today is your last day, and you will be the happiest person on the planet when your last day finally comes.

Remember this important Secret on Success Goals and Mindset: *Get out of your comfort zone.*

Secret #11

Learn to Manage Your Fears

To become a multi-millionaire, you must reduce or eliminate fear from your life. Fear holds people back from achieving greatness.

F - False
E - Evidence
A - Appearing
R – Real

Common fears that hold child care center owners back:

Fear of failure: This stems from childhood for most people as we are afraid to disappoint people, most of all ourselves. You may have a negative view of yourself and feel that you may not be good enough to accomplish your goal, so you tend to err on the side of caution when goals and dreams are set.

Fear of change: Change is hard. You don't know what you don't know, and change brings uncertainty, which scares most people. The only constant in life is change, so it is time to embrace change as an opportunity for growth. It takes about 21 days to form a new habit, so do what you are afraid to do, and eventually, it becomes less scary.

Fear of success: Yes, there is such a thing. Some people think so little of themselves that they will sabotage their businesses for fear of succeeding. It is more common than people think and is one of the biggest reasons why there are so few multi-center owners.

Fear of what others will think of you: Social media has exasperated this fear, as we are always concerned about our appearance to others. Being a business owner, you are in the minority, and there is a good chance that you are the only one in your family. People mock what they do not understand, so you may have been laughed at for your goals and dreams before. If people are not laughing at your goals and dreams, **THEY ARE NOT BIG ENOUGH!**

Book Recommendation:
How to Stop Worrying and Start Living
by Dale Carnegie

We were laughed at when we started our child care business. We were laughed at when we launched our real estate management business. We were told by friends that we would not succeed with some of our expansion plans. We were criticized for working so hard to build our dreams. When we were in the Navy, we told people we would be multi-millionaire business owners one day, and they all laughed. Guess who's laughing now?

Success has a way of enacting revenge that is so bittersweet! What fears are holding you back? In the next Secret, we will be setting some goals and dreams for you, we have to first let these fears go, or we won't be able to hit these goals.

Let's take a moment and write what we feel is holding us back:

My biggest fear is:

_____

_____

_____

I will do this to ensure that this fear does not keep me from my goals:

_____

_____

_____

_____

_____

_____

Remember this important Secret on Success Goals and Mindset: ***Learn to manage your fears.***

Secret #12

Set Detailed Stretch Goals

To become a multi-millionaire, you must have a specific plan. When climbing a mountain, the higher you climb, the further you can see. As you start working on your goals and dreams, you will be able to see a clearer picture of how your business will grow over time. Let's set some long-term goals for our business.

2-year plan: on _____ (add date) I will have the following:

_____ locations

_____ employees

$_____ in gross annual revenue

$_____ in net annual income

$_____ value of real estate owned

5-year plan: on _____ (add date) I will have the following:

      _____ locations
      _____ employees
      $_____ in gross annual revenue
      $_____ in net annual income
      $_____ value of real estate owned

10-year plan: on _____ (add date) I will have the following:

      _____ locations
      _____ employees
      $_____ in gross annual revenue
      $_____ in net annual income
      $_____ value of real estate owned

20-year plan: on _____ (add date) I will have the following:

      _____ locations
      _____ employees
      $_____ in gross annual revenue
      $_____ in net annual income
      $_____ value of real estate owned

Only 3% of business owners write down their goals. Would you like to guess what percentage of business owners achieve their goals and dreams...3%!

Writing down your goals and placing them where you can see them every day will increase your chances of success. Place yellow sticky notes with your goals around your office, on your bathroom mirror, on the ceiling above your bed, on your speedometer, below your computer monitor, above the toilet paper holder, and just about anywhere you can see and think of them often. You are conditioning your subconscious for success.

What are some other goals for your business? What are some dreams of yours? New house, car, debt free, kids college fund, etc.

Let's write some short and long-term goals and dreams you would like to accomplish:

1. _____

2. _____

3. _____

4. _____

5. _____

6. _____

7. _____

8. _____

9. _____

10. _____

Congratulations on taking the first step to achieving your goals and dreams. Having your goals in front of you will allow you to put your plans into motion and help you to achieve anything in life you can dream of; the only limits are the ones you place on yourself.

Remember this important Secret on Success Goals and Mindset: *Set detailed stretch goals.*

Secret #13

Consistency is the Key to Long-Term Success

Being consistent with all things is the most important key to success. Consistency in your attitude and actions will make you a multi-millionaire in the fastest way possible. The Secret to your long-term success is exposed in your daily routine. Let's create some daily routines that will be life-changing.

Reading: Read 15-30 minutes daily in a positive mental attitude (PMA) book.

Book Recommendation:
The Slight Edge
by Jeff Olson

Visioning: Closing your eyes and picturing yourself with your goals already obtained. When you see an Olympic runner close their eyes before the race, they envision themselves crossing the finish line first. Visioning allows your brain to see the result of your consistent action; it will motivate you more.

Action: Work on something that advances your goals and dreams every day. A little bit each day will accomplish a lot in a year.

Habits: Create good work, sleep, health, and family time habits that you are proud of. Find the balance between work and home life and create a consistent action plan.

Gratitude: Write something you are thankful for every day in your gratitude journal.

Brain food: Listen to positive podcasts or audiobooks while commuting to feed your brain positive thoughts.

Pray: If you are a spiritual person, make a habit of giving thanks and asking for wisdom and guidance.

Health: Exercise and eat healthily consistently. Avoid crash diets and intense workouts. Slow and steady wins the health race.

Remember this important Secret on Success Goals and Mindset: ***Consistency is the key to long-term success.***

Secret #14

Join the Child Care Mindset Facebook Group

You and your staff deal with a lot of negativity every day. We have created a positive resource for you on Facebook where you and your team members can get an uplifting message of encouragement to make your day a little brighter.

Visit Facebook.com/groups/childcaremindset and request to join. Anyone who owns or works in a child care setting is free to join. Please send all of your team members here as well. They are bombarded with negativity on Facebook, but at least you know they will get a little bit of positivity in their day.

Remember this important Secret on Success Goals and Mindset: ***Join the Child Care Mindset Facebook group.***

Secret #15

Positive Self-Talk Only

This is the final Secret to Success Goals and Mindset. This is the longest chapter for one reason, without goals and the proper mindset you will NEVER become a multi-millionaire.

This Secret is one of the most important ones. It has the power to cause you to achieve your goals and dreams, and it also has the ability to sabotage everything that you are working for.

Have you ever called yourself a dummy, an idiot, ugly, or maybe a fool? Have you ever said to yourself, "I cannot do that," when faced with a task at hand? When doubt creeps into your head, it is the self-talk that is causing you to second guess your abilities.

> ### Book Recommendation:
> ### *What to Say When You Talk to Your Self*
> by Shad Helmstetter.

You must believe you can succeed. Your brain does not know the difference between the truth and a lie; it will believe what it is programmed to believe. If you keep telling yourself you are a winner; you are awesome, you are beautiful, you are smart, you are amazing, you are giving, you are caring, you will begin to believe it. Your brain will then start working at manifesting these thoughts into reality.

Place positive sticky notes everywhere around your home. Your brain will see them. Write the note as if you have already achieved it.

I weigh 125 pounds. I eat healthily. I am a winner. I am a multi-millionaire. I own 10 profitable centers. You get the idea. Fill your brain with positive thoughts and read these notes aloud as often as possible. You are brainwashing yourself for success instead of letting society condition you for failure.

It will initially seem weird, and your family members will laugh when they hear you talking to yourself. Stay consistent; it will pay off. There is power in the spoken word. *"You are snared by the words of your mouth."* ~ Proverbs 6:2

Remember this important Secret on Success Goals and Mindset: ***Positive self-talk only.***

Chapter 1 Notes

Chapter 2

Corporate Structure

"I'm a true believer in the strength of teamwork, in the power of dreams, and in the absolute necessity of a support structure."
~ Julie Payette

Now that you have your mindset and long-term goals, let's start building that multi-million-dollar business.

Having the right corporate structure when your business is small will help you to scale it without making major changes along the way. There are many ways to set up the corporate structure of your corporation, so please speak with your accountant, as this person knows your business and your particular situation the best.

Do not wait until your business is big to treat it like it is big. We were multi-millionaires in our minds long before it showed up on paper. We used the same corporate structure with seven locations as we did with just one.

Secret #16

Have the Right Tax Structure

Having the proper tax and liability structure is vital to protecting your business and paying the least taxes allowed. The type of structure is up to you and depends on many factors. The different types of setups are listed below, with a brief overview of what they accomplish. Consult your tax advisor and attorney for advice specific to your situation.

The Small Business Administration is a great resource for setting up a corporation, be sure to visit their website at sba.gov. These are the types of Corporations you can form; the definitions are provided by the Small Business Administration:

Sole Proprietorship: A sole proprietorship is easy to form and gives you complete control of your business. You're automatically considered a sole proprietorship if you do business activities but don't register as any other kind of business.

Sole proprietorships do not produce a separate business entity. This means your business assets and liabilities are not separate from your personal assets and liabilities. You can be held personally liable for the debts and obligations of the business. Sole proprietors are still able to get a trade name. It can also be hard to raise money because you can't sell the stock, and banks are hesitant to lend to sole proprietorships.

Sole proprietorships can be a good choice for low-risk businesses and owners who want to test their business idea before forming a more formal business.

Partnership: Partnerships are the simplest structure for two or more people to own a business together. There are two common kinds of partnerships: limited partnerships (LP) and limited liability partnerships (LLP).

Limited partnerships have only one general partner with unlimited liability, and all other partners have limited liability. The partners with limited liability also tend to have limited control over the company, which is documented in a partnership agreement. Profits are passed through to personal tax returns, and the general partner — the partner without limited liability — must also pay self-employment taxes.

Limited liability partnerships are similar to limited partnerships, but give limited liability to every owner. An LLP protects each partner from debts against the partnership; they won't be responsible for the actions of other partners.

Partnerships can be a good choice for businesses with multiple owners, professional groups (like attorneys), and groups who want to test their business idea before forming a more formal business.

Limited liability company (LLC): An LLC lets you take advantage of the benefits of both the corporation and partnership business structures.

LLCs protect you from personal liability in most instances; your personal assets — like your vehicle, house, and savings accounts — won't be at risk in case your LLC faces bankruptcy or lawsuits.

Profits and losses can get passed through to your personal income without facing corporate taxes. However, members of an LLC are considered self-employed and must pay self-employment tax contributions toward Medicare and Social Security.

LLCs can have a limited life in many states. When a member joins or leaves an LLC, some states may require the LLC to be dissolved and re-formed with new membership — unless there's already an agreement within the LLC for buying, selling, and transferring ownership.

LLCs can be a good choice for medium- or higher-risk businesses, owners with significant personal assets they want to be protected, and owners who want to pay a lower tax rate than a corporation.

Corporations

C corp: A corporation, sometimes called a C corp, is a legal entity separate from its owners. Corporations can make a profit, be taxed, and can be held legally liable.

Corporations offer the strongest protection to their owners from personal liability, but the cost to form a corporation is higher than other structures. Corporations also require more extensive record-keeping, operational processes, and reporting.

Unlike sole proprietors, partnerships, and LLCs, corporations pay income tax on their profits. In some cases, corporate profits are taxed twice — first, when the company makes a profit, and again when dividends are paid to shareholders on their personal tax returns.

Corporations have a completely independent life separate from their shareholders. If a shareholder leaves the company or sells shares, the C corp can continue doing business relatively undisturbed.

Corporations have an advantage when it comes to raising capital because they can raise funds through the sale of stock, which can also be a benefit in attracting employees.

Corporations can be a good choice for medium- or higher-risk businesses, those that need to raise money, and businesses that plan to "go public" or eventually be sold.

S corp: An S corporation, sometimes called an S corp, is a special type designed to avoid the double taxation drawback of regular C corps. S corps allow profits, and some losses, to be passed through directly to owners' personal income without ever being subject to corporate tax rates.

Not all states tax S corps equally, but most recognize them the same way the federal government does and tax the shareholders accordingly. Some states tax S corps on profits above a specified limit, and others don't recognize the S corp election, simply treating the business as a C corp.

S corps must file with the IRS to get S corp status, a different process from registering with their state.

There are special limits on S corps. Check the IRS website for eligibility requirements.

You'll still have to follow the strict filing and operational processes of a C corp.

S corps also have an independent life, just like C corps. If a shareholder leaves the company or sells shares, the S corp can continue doing business relatively undisturbed.

S corps can be a good choice for businesses that would otherwise be a C corp, but meet the criteria to file as an S corp.

Nonprofit corporation: Nonprofit corporations are organized to do charity, education, religious, literary, or scientific work. Because their work benefits the public, nonprofits can receive tax-exempt status, meaning they don't pay state or federal income taxes on any profits.

Nonprofits must file with the IRS to get tax exemption, a different process from registering with their state.

Nonprofit corporations need to follow organizational rules very similar to regular C corp. They also need to follow special rules about what they do with any profits they earn. For example, they can't distribute profits to members or political campaigns.

Nonprofits are often called 501(c)(3) corporations — a reference to the section of the Internal Revenue Code that is most commonly used to grant tax-exempt status.

We have seen every different structure used and will not criticize anyone for what they do. There are so many factors to consider that as long as your CPA and Attorney are on board, we won't criticize it. If you are not getting advice from professionals and instead are relying on what someone else has done or what a relative suggests, then we will criticize you.

We have had some owners have a separate corporation for each location. While there are some legal benefits to having separate corporate ownership, having the proper amount of insurance should suffice in case of legal problems. Think of every major corporation in America; they are all just one company.

There is an argument for owning the property in an LLC separate from your child care business. Every property we own is a separate LLC, but they are considered pass-through entities and do not have to file a separate tax return. Get with your CPA for the best way to protect yourself and your assets.

Remember this important Secret on Corporate Structure: *Have the right tax structure.*

Secret #17

Establish a Leadership Team

Depending on the current size of your child care business, you will want to establish a "leadership team" early on. These are your trusted advisors. If you own one center and have a director, then you both will be on the leadership team.

As you open more centers, your leadership team will grow. In our company, we have two teams, an admin team and a leadership team.

Our admin team is made up of owners and the executive director only. This way, top-level decisions can be made privately based on the company's needs.

Our leadership team comprises the owners, all of our directors, and our executive director. You can bring your assistant director(s) to your leadership team if you wish, but try not to get the meeting to more than 10 people; it gets harder to manage.

If you have more than 10 centers, we recommend splitting them into different leadership teams by geographical area. The executive director would be responsible for overseeing the multiple leadership teams.

We recommend getting the entire company leadership together once or twice a year in person so networking and learning can take place between the groups. You can do team-building activities to strengthen camaraderie and morale.

Everyone on the leadership team needs to know the importance of confidentiality and accountability. What happens on the LT stays on the LT!

Remember this important Secret on Corporate Structure: *Establish a leadership team.*

Secret #18

Schedule Weekly Leadership Meetings

Most people do not like meetings. Child care owners and directors thrive in the fast-paced environment of child care center life, and a meeting seems like you are working in slow motion. It is not liked by many in child care leadership.

Weekly meetings are very important for many reasons. They bring accountability through reporting metrics that will be tracked. They will also shed light on problems at the center that can be problematic. Virtual meetings are preferred if you have more than one location.

Having every person be able to speak and provide input, where their voice is heard and valued, is the key to making meetings a place where everyone wants to be there. No one wants to be lectured at a meeting; everyone wants to feel they can speak without fear or intimidation.

Each meeting should have an agenda and always start and end on time. We recommend including the following in each meeting:

- Intro Time - 1-2 minutes where each person discusses what is going on in their life personally and professionally. This relaxes the participants and lets them know you care about them as a person.
- Issues and potential problems - This is where members bring up issues that concern the Leadership Team. These issues are then discussed until the problem is resolved with input from everyone that wishes to speak.
- Numbers - The directors bring items that the LT wants to track. (# of tours, # of inquiries, # of new enrolled, # of withdrawals, Amount of non-payments, etc). Feel free to track any number you wish, just be sure to track them on a spreadsheet to compare weekly. If numbers are slipping, it can become a problem that the group discusses how to improve on.

- Project List - What people are currently working on.
- Wrap-up - The meeting leader summarizes the meeting, reiterates the action items, and wishes everyone a fantastic week.

Feel free to structure your meeting however you wish, keeping in mind that the more your team members feel comfortable, the more they will share. The more they share, the faster your team will grow. As an owner, please don't be a dictator; allow your people to have an equal voice taking in all sides of an argument. They will respect you for listening, even if you do not agree with them.

Remember this important Secret on Corporate Structure: *Schedule weekly leadership meetings.*

Secret #19

Have an Accountability Chart

Who is responsible for tours at your center? Who is responsible for a follow-up? How about training new staff? There are hundreds of different responsibilities in a child care dynasty that someone needs to be responsible and accountable for; this is why we create an accountability chart.

An accountability chart is a flowchart that lists the employees and what responsibilities they are accountable for. It should be updated regularly and posted where employees can see it. With each responsibility, there should be a manual of core processes which we will cover in the next Secret.

Once you create the accountability chart, be sure to make a copy of it and share it with all employees represented in the chart. This way, they know what their responsibilities are and what they are accountable for.

Remember this important Secret on Corporate Structure: *Have an accountability chart.*

Secret #20

Have a Core Processes Manual

There are eight main core processes to most multi-center child care programs, so we recommend you begin with these, and you can always add more if your particular structure calls for it.
We establish the main core processes and then detail the exact procedures used. This way, team members in your accountability chart know what processes they are responsible and accountable for and exactly how they should be done.

The majority of child care dynasties will need the following eight core processes. We have included some examples of some of the sub-processes. It is up to you to write up the details of the process and who is accountable for the process.

Company Leadership Processes
- Leadership team meeting schedule
- Communication
- Accountability chart
- Scorecard

Marketing Processes
- Advertising
- Social media
- Newsletter
- Website
- Branding

Tour Processes
- Phone scripts and procedures
- Tour procedures
- Follow-up routine

Center Processes
- Cleaning
- Maintenance
- IT

Customer Management Processes
- Customer retention
- Billing and tuition collection
- Parent communication app
- Regulatory Compliance Processes
- State licensing
- Ratio compliance
- Licensing violations

Employee and Human Resources Processes
- Hiring and termination
- Federal and state compliance
- Wage increase procedures
- Onboarding
- Benefits administration
- Employee recognition
- Job descriptions

Finance Processes
- Reports
- Budget - department and company
- Cash flow
- Accounts payable
- Accounts receivable
- Reconciliation

This is by no means a complete list. Your business may have more or fewer processes and more or fewer sub-processes. Use this list above merely as a place to start from.

When you finish writing your core processes, place them in an online document and share it with all of your leadership team members. Be sure everyone reads them and signs that they have read them and will abide by them. All employees in leadership must know the company's core processes and who is accountable for them. Let them know that suggestions are welcome to improve any process.

Remember this important Secret on Corporate Structure: **Have a core processes manual.**

Secret #21

Keep a Weekly Numbers Spreadsheet

If you are not tracking critical numbers in your organization, you have no way of knowing if you are growing or shrinking. Measuring is the only proper way to know.

Historical data is essential to an organization and will help you predict trends over time. For instance, our organization has tracked full and part-time enrollment numbers for over 14 years. Knowing what months historically have increased enrollment helps you to plan on staffing a few weeks before you need the staff. Most owners react to changes in enrollment by hiring more. With historical data, you can hire the teachers before you need them (and before your competitors hire them) so they will be fully trained when you need them.

There are many numbers you can track weekly, and they can be discussed at your weekly meeting. Directors can be responsible for enrollment numbers, full and part-time, of each classroom.

They can also be responsible for tracking employee attendance, hiring, and terminations. Anything you want to track from your center, your director can bring to a meeting; just be sure to log the information.

Owners may also want to track weekly or monthly tuition received, tuition in arrears, the number of subsidized children, total staff (full and part-time), social media likes or follows, leads received, tours given, tour conversion rates, total enrollments, and withdrawals, etc. The more you track, the better picture of the health of your business you will have.

Remember this important Secret on Corporate Structure: ***Keep a weekly numbers spreadsheet.***

Secret #22

Track Your FTE Enrollment

FTE stands for Full-Time Equivalent. It is very important to always know your FTE, and it should be tracked weekly, placed on a spreadsheet, and kept for many years. This historical data is very important.

If you have 50 full-time and ten part-time children at your center, how many FTE is that?

If you have 40 full-time and 20 part-time children, how many FTE is that?

In the above examples, which would you rather have? 50 full/10 part or 40 full/20 part?

Your answer should be it depends on the tuition structure.

At our school, we break part-time down based on hours attending. Over 30 hours is full-time, 20-30 hours is part-time, 10-20 hours is half-time, and under 10 hours is quarter-time.

A part-time student counts as .75 FTE, a half-time student counts as .5 FTE, and a quarter-time student counts as .25 FTE.

Let's say you have 50 full-time and ten quarter-time students.

50 - full-time is 50 FTE

10 - quarter-time is 2.5 FTE

In the above example, the center has 60 children enrolled and an FTE of 52.5.

Now let's look at a center with 40 full-time children, 15 part-time children, and five half-time children.

40 - full-time is 40 FTE

15 - part-time is 11.25 FTE

5 - half-time is 2.5 FTE

In the above example, the center has 60 children enrolled and an FTE of 53.75.

Both schools have 60 children enrolled, but the center with fewer full-time children makes more money. Knowing your FTE allows you to always have an apples-to-apples comparison of the revenue, regardless of the fluctuations in full- and part-time children. Always keep and track your FTE weekly, monthly, and annually; it will never let you down.

Remember this important Secret on Corporate Structure: ***Track your FTE enrollment.***

Secret #23

Consider Centralized Leads and Tours

If you have more than three centers, you may wish to consider centralizing your leads and tours. We started with an "Enrollment Manager" about six years ago, which has made a huge difference in our tour conversions and profitability.

We had five centers at the time and five different directors doing five different types of tours and five different tour conversion rates. We had five people all answering calls and setting up tours, all with varying degrees of success.

We then decided to try to take our best tour converter and have her handle all the leads and tours. She would talk to each lead on the phone, set up all tours, and spend one day at each school weekly doing tours. If someone came in for a walk-in tour, the onsite director would handle it (unless the enrollment manager was at the school that day). She would also do all follow-ups and send initial enrollment paperwork and collect initial tuition for all new students. She was also responsible for managing our CRM system, which tracked our leads and tours.

By moving to this model, our tour conversions improved, profitability increased, directors had more time to manage their staff and the school, and everyone was much happier. The extra salary for this position was more than made up by the increased enrollment, and it was a win-win for all involved.

We recommend that your "enrollment manager" handles up to five locations, and when you grow larger, you need to hire another one. Five seems to be the magic number, providing all locations are within 2 hours of each other.

Remember this important Secret on Corporate Structure: *Consider centralized leads and tours.*

Secret #24

Delegate to Liberate

Our job at Child Care Genius is to give you tools to help you to work smarter, not harder. One of the ways you can work smarter is to delegate. Delegation liberates you from overworking and getting burned out before you have reaped the financial benefits of long-term business ownership.

Ask yourself: Am I more comfortable in a classroom or an office? If you said classroom, you are a teacher at heart, and office work is secondary in your mind. If you said office, you think like a businessperson who happens to own a daycare.

Business people are typically better at delegating because they feel they cannot do everything themselves. If you are a teacher at heart, you have an overabundance of empathy and can feel guilty when asking someone else to do something you are capable of doing; this leads to an overworking of the owner because they feel they have to always be there or the center will fall apart.

You need to take some extra time to learn to delegate. There are exceptions to this, of course, but for the most part, this is what we have witnessed in our 25 years in the industry.

Book Recommendation:
How to Influence People
by Dr. John C. Maxwell

As an owner, you have to be able to delegate a lot of responsibilities to other staff members, an assistant director, a director, or possibly an executive director, depending on your size. If you do not learn to do this, how will you ever take a day off, a vacation, or maternity leave?

Delegation is liberation. If you want to be free to live your life and have a life outside of the child care center, it is vital that you learn to delegate. If you have someone you trust, start by getting out of your school one day a week. If that is too much, try a half day. If that is too much, try lunch. Baby step your way up to more and more time away. The more you can work on your business instead of in your business, the more successful you will be. Some of the most successful owners we have met spend less than an hour a week at their schools.

Remember this important Secret on Corporate Structure: ***Delegate to liberate.***

Chapter 2 Notes

Chapter 3

Corporate Leadership

"If your actions inspire others to dream more, learn more, do more, and become more, you are a leader."
~ John Quincy Adams

So far, we have worked on our mindset, goals, and corporate structure, and it is time to start developing corporate leadership. To build an extensive child care program, you need to think and act differently than you did early on in your business.

There is a difference in the leadership required to build a sizable multi-center child care business. As we like to say, what got you here won't get you there. We have seen some accidental child care successes, those who don't know what they are doing stumble into a child care business that makes seven figures. Many owners have bought million-dollar companies and hit seven figures in year one; that's not very impressive. When you start with no kids and create seven figures, that is more impressive.

It takes leadership to build a child care dynasty with which very few people are born. Leadership is learned through books, courses, podcasts, and experience. It is not easy to build a child care dynasty; that is probably why most center owners have one center (it's easier to run five schools than one, they just don't know that yet because they have not finished this book!).

This next chapter may bloody your nose a little bit, but that is okay. As we said before, we are not out to make friends; we are here to help you build a sizable multi-center operation. We have not written anything in this book that we did not do ourselves in building our child care dynasty; that makes us different from many child care coaches. We have done what we write about and teach.

Secret #25

Develop Strong Leadership Skills

Leaders are not born; they are developed. We are both U.S. Navy Veterans, and leadership is critical to the U.S. military. So much so that they spend a lot of time and money investing in the leadership of the men and women in the military. We have both been to leadership school, where we learned to lead other people. Leadership is influence, plain and simple.

We weren't born leaders; we were made leaders. We took what we learned from the military and then built upon that with books, tapes, and training. We became students again, following John Maxwell and devouring his leadership books. We later became John Maxwell certified coaches, masters of his leadership techniques.

You are not alone if you were never taught to lead; most child care center owners and directors have no formal leadership training. This is good news; with a bit of training and guidance, you can be well on your way to becoming a dominating leader in your market. Everyone wants to follow and work for a genuine leader who remains calm when things get tough. As John Maxwell says about business, "everything rises and falls on leadership."

Reading leadership books is the best way to develop the leadership skills necessary to learn what you need to know to grow your child care dynasty to greatness. Taking a little time out of your day to build your leadership skills will yield incredible results down the road, but it takes discipline.

We have a recommended reading section on our website at ChildCareGenius.com/resources with a leadership books section; this is a great place to start.

If you find it hard to find time to read, try an audiobook, and listen to it during your morning and evening commutes or while you are working out. We all have 24 hours a day; how we use that time separates the winners from the losers.

Remember this important Secret on Corporate Leadership: *Develop strong leadership skills.*

Secret #26

Develop the Leaders on Your Team

By developing the leaders on your team, you can start allowing the business to run without you being involved in every little decision. There is an art to proper delegation; we will give you a few pointers.

Without leaders on your team, you will never build a child care dynasty; it is simply not possible. The more quality leaders you have, the faster you will grow. Leave your ego at the door; you want the leaders on your team to do EVERYTHING better than you do.

Never get upset when parents like them more or the staff would rather have them around; that is a great thing. Since you cannot be in two places at once, and you will want to take vacations often, as I stated in an earlier Secret, you must trust your leaders to lead in your absence.

Be precise: There is nothing worse you can do to the leaders on your team than give them unclear guidance on how to complete a task. Be sure to spell out the how, what, when, where and why so they know exactly what is expected of them. Doing this will make everyone very happy in the long run.

Don't micromanage: Give them the project and get out of their way. Allow them to figure things out on their own, and also allow them to fail a little. Nothing is a better learning experience than a mistake.

Give feedback: If there were things done incorrectly, do not get upset. Make sure the directions are clear and let them know what needs to be fixed and when you would like it done. Keep

58

repeating until you are satisfied with the project's completion. When they do a great job, be sure to tell them so. A compliment goes a long way in having that person want to do an even better job in the future.

Train them: Send them to leadership training and buy them leadership books. Encourage them to develop their leadership skills and reward them for becoming a leader on your team.

Have patience: Not everyone is born to lead, but some take more time than others. Be willing to train, retrain, and retrain again. They may have to take many courses and read many books. After all that, some people just won't have what it takes. You will know they are not cut out for the job when they try to lead, and no one is following.

Book Recommendation:
The 21 Indispensable Qualities of a Leader
by Dr. John C. Maxwell

Remember this important Secret on Corporate Leadership*:*
Develop the leaders on your team.

Secret #27

Develop Your Future Leaders

You need to start developing future leaders now. Look for employees that you think are future leaders and start investing in giving them leadership training now. These people will be your future assistant directors, future directors, and future assistant directors. These future leaders are your management trainees.

They need to know they are being groomed to be a future leader on your team when a spot opens up.

We have opened ten schools over the last 24 years and have only hired one director that wasn't already on staff (this was our first director at our first school). Since then, we have only promoted directors from within our team, where we developed them sometimes for years.

When you hire a director off the street, it can take a long time for them to fit into your culture. The staff may take a while to adjust, and they may never adjust to them. We had seen many directors who were great at one center and flop when they went to a new school.

We never wanted to be in the position of a staff member having leverage over us. By having 2-3 qualified directors that can take over at a moment's notice, we never had to worry when a director gave notice. What would happen at your school if your director quit today without notice?

Many years ago, we had two directors quit on the same day, and they were replaced the next day without skipping a beat. Most owners would have freaked out; we were as calm as possible and immediately worked on building our future leadership team.

We would estimate that 90% of the directors we have promoted never saw themselves as a director; we sought them out and developed them and worked on their confidence and belief that they could lead people and make a more significant difference on the planet. We didn't make them leaders; we opened the door for them to develop their leadership ability because we saw they had what it takes, even before they knew.

Not everyone works out; this is why your future leadership team needs to be a deep bench. Some may never be called up to serve in leadership, but that is okay. They can do great things in helping your junior staff develop.

Remember this important Secret on Corporate Leadership: **Develop your future leaders.**

Secret #28

Learn From Your Mistakes
(and the Mistakes of Others)

Show us someone who has made no mistakes, and we will show you a loser. Mistakes are a necessary part of life; without them, we would never have learned anything.

When we were learning to walk, our parents let us fall. They were not being cruel; they wanted our brains to know what failure felt like. Failure hurts, and our brain learns quickly to avoid that hurt and learn to do it the less painful way.

There are two ways in life to learn. You can learn from your own mistakes, or you can learn from the mistakes of others. We can promise you that it is much cheaper and less painful to learn from the mistakes of others.

One day we got a call from a hospital in a town about 20 minutes away. It was a small hospital in a very rural area in a small town. They asked us to open a child care center next door to the hospital for staff to use for child care. They bought us a building and renovated it; then they leased it back to us.

We were excited to open a new location until we realized we weren't profitable after year one. We could not understand why doctors and nurses were not enrolling their children; we made it so convenient for them to be next door to the hospital.

We failed to do our market research before opening. We assumed doctors and nurses would like the convenience of having their children so close, but that was not the case.

On average, the doctors and nurses at this hospital lived 30 miles away and had a 40-60 minute commute twice a day (depending on Maine weather). They wanted to drop their child off at a child care facility close to their house and have a quiet, child-free commute to work, and when they got off of work, they wanted a calm commute home until they had to pick up their child and have a noisy five-minute drive home from daycare.

We spent several years at that location, never made a profit, and closed the center. Was it a failure? No. We learned that before you open a site, do detailed market research and never assume anything.

Take this story and learn from our mistakes, which is way smarter than making the same mistake yourself. The more you hang out with child care leaders, the more you learn from their mistakes. This is the power of the Child Care Genius University, which you will learn about later.

Book Recommendation:
Sometimes You Win, Sometimes You Learn
by Dr. John C. Maxwell

The best question you can ever ask a successful child care center owner is this: "What is the biggest mistake you made in building your business?" You will learn far more from that answer than asking the person about their most significant success.

There are two ways to make money in business. One is to make money, and one is to avoid losing money. Learning from the mistakes of others allows us to keep from losing money in the future, which is money in the bank that you would have lost had you not learned the lesson beforehand.

Remember this important Secret on Corporate Leadership: *Learn from your mistakes (and the mistakes of others).*

Secret #29

Perfection is Not Possible

No one is perfect. We all make mistakes, and those mistakes give us life lessons to learn and grow from. The more successful you are, the more mistakes you have made along the way.

We have seen many owners over the years that are perfectionists. The perfectionist owner is typically a control freak who has difficulty delegating and letting go. Things have to be done a certain way, and if it is not done exactly right, it is 100% wrong in their eyes.

In our partnership, Brian was the perfectionist. Things had to be done Brian's way, and any deviation would cause anxiety and stress for Brian and a feeling of a loss of control. In his eyes, no one could do things the way he wanted them done; therefore, he had a hard time delegating.

It took years for Brian to realize that being a perfectionist was not only holding his business back but also creating health problems with too much stress and anxiety.

Learning to delegate and trust others is hard for someone who likes control, but essential if you are ever to grow your business past the point of ten employees. An owner can have total control of up to about ten employees, but once you start getting more, you will have to start learning to delegate.

The first step to perfectionist recovery is learning to accept other people's imperfections. When you assign a project to someone, and they give 100% to the project, even if it is only 90% of what you would accomplish, you have to learn to accept that standard as good enough.

NO ONE will ever give your business more focus than you; you are the one that knows the big picture. You can see things no one else sees. You are privy to seeing the whole business plan in your head, so when a project is given to someone, they do not know 100% of what you know, so why would they be able to do something 100% as good as you would do it?

If an owner has OCD, this can be an even more significant challenge. Someone with OCD has a major problem with a lack of organization, and delegation that is not in line with the organization can cause significant problems. We recommend having written processes for projects that can be followed to the letter, which will help.

The best thing we did for our business was to separate duties. Brian took over the financials, which are the one area of your business that you need a perfectionist to look after, Carol took over as the head of operations overseeing staff and marketing. Since this is where 95% of the delegation took place, this worked well for us. Don't be afraid to hire someone and put them in charge of the delegation if you lack the skills to deal with imperfect people regularly.

If you are a perfectionist, we feel your pain. The good news is that you can work around it and build a very successful business as we have; you have to be patient and apologize a lot! Be sure to let employees know your weaknesses and allow them to find a way that you can work together.

If you have a therapist, ask this person to help you with delegation and living with imperfection. Most trained therapists will have exercises you can do and help you put a plan together to help you grow. We promise that once you get this behind you, nothing will stop you from climbing on board the success train. Remember that imperfect people in an imperfect world built the success train.

Remember this important Secret on Corporate Leadership: **Perfection is not possible.**

Secret #30

Become a Good Time Manager

We know that everyone has 24 hours in a day. Why does it seem like some people can do so much more than we can with their time? Why do you see some child care center owners who vacation every few months, and you haven't had one in years? How do they do it? They have become masters of time management.

It all starts with figuring out your strengths and weaknesses. What do you love to do? What do you dislike doing? What can you pay someone else to do so you can work on higher payoff activities?

Delegation allows you to spend time on the things you are good at (and want to do) and delegate everything else to someone good at those things. You should ensure you do not work more than 40 hours per week, 48 weeks per year. Doing that will keep you balanced and not get burned out. Delegate enough to find that work "sweet spot." Once you have delegation mastered, you can add more vacation time and dial back your work hours to 30 or less if you want to.

If you choose to expand your business by adding additional locations, be sure to protect your time by delegating to ensure you do not add additional work hours as your business scales. Each time we added a location, we ensured we worked less after it opened to account for the other responsibilities we needed for more downtime. This has worked out very well for us over the last 25 years.

Decide to get control of your calendar, and you will be able to repurchase your life. Your center will run fine without you, and your team will more than likely perform better when you are not there to micro-manage them. The more you work from home, the easier this will be. They won't know whether you are working or not when you are not at the center.

Remember this important Secret on Corporate Leadership: ***Become a good time manager.***

Secret #31

Team-Based Core Values are Important

A team's core values tell the world what your employee's deep-down held work beliefs are. That is something that should come from them and not from the ownership of the business.

The more you can get your team involved in creating the center's core values, the more they will be invested in ensuring that their co-workers live up to the values. You can hire, fire, and train your team solely on the core values that the group helps to create.

Creating or re-creating a team's core values will take a few hours, but the positive effects will last for years. Your mission is to guide your team but have little say over the overall outcome.

Book Recommendation:
Built on Values
by Ann Rhoades

Get your entire team together and go through a core values creation exercise by brainstorming ideas and looking for 1-3 word phrases. (FUN, FAMILY, TEAMWORK, LOVE CHILDREN, PASSION, INTEGRITY, etc.).

Allow everyone to yell them out and write them all on a giant board. After all of them are written down, it is time for the team members to vote. We made each person with the most extended hair the table captain, and each person wrote the three they liked on a piece of paper. The table captain then adds them together and waits for each table to finish.

Once all tables are finished, the table captain reads the count to the person on the mainboard, and they make a mark next to each vote. This continues until all of the tables have given you their favorites.

Circle the top five values, and they become your company's core values if there is a tie between five and six, simply vote between the two to find who takes the fifth spot. (This example assumes five core values, the most common number).

The following exercise is to define what your core values are. Each table can work independently on them and develop an up to ten-word phrase that describes the core value. FUN - *We make learning fun at Little Angels!*

66

Each table comes up with a phrase for each core value, and then they are voted on by everyone, and the one with the most votes is the phrase you use. When done, allow audience members to make suggestions if they have suggestions for refining anything further, and always re-vote to make sure everyone agrees.

When we did this exercise, we, as owners, did not vote nor have any input whatsoever. We just watched it happen. Our employees owned their values, and still live up to them today after many years.

Do not be afraid to let employees make their values; you will be surprised at how good they will do, and we promise they will come up with better ones than you can. After all, they live these values daily in working for you and the children.

Remember this important Secret on Corporate Leadership: **Team-based core values are important.**

Secret #32

Be a Positive (Neutral) Role Model

at all Times

As the owner of a child care business, you have an incredible responsibility to ensure that you are a positive role model for the employees at your school, the children who attend, and the parents that trust you. You also have the responsibility to be a neutral party in areas where there may be differing opinions.

You will have employees and parents from every race, religion, ethnicity, sexual orientation, political party, and ideology attending, and you have to remain a neutral party in all correspondence.

Switzerland is a neutral country and did not take sides in WWII. To this day, Switzerland is considered a neutral country. You need to be like Switzerland when it comes to political debates.

You will get canceled quickly in today's society for saying the wrong thing; it could take years to recover from it. Remaining neutral is one way to avoid the cancel culture from canceling your school, and either side of a debate can cancel you quickly.

We never posted political signs on our daycare property nor permitted candidates to do so. Not because we did not have a favorite, but because we did not want our employees or parents to feel different about us for our beliefs because we did not care about theirs. No one has ever voted for someone based on a political sign; they are a complete waste of money.

We kept our social media posts neutral and did not criticize our employees for exercising their rights to self-expression. We tell our employees to respect those they disagree with because you are all on the same team, the kids' team! Have you ever changed your mind about anything based on what you saw on social media? We doubt it!

When you are in public, watch what you do. The community is watching you. Don't drink and drive. Don't do drugs or abuse alcohol. Don't have the police called to your house. Be a model member of society. Everyone is looking for an excuse to talk wrong about someone, don't let that gossip be about you.

Have one on one conversations with your team members annually. Get to know them, and be a positive influence in their lives. Be sure to be close enough to them that they will come to you when they are in trouble, but not so tight that the boundary between employer and employee gets crossed. It is a fine line.

Be sure to let employees know you are always there for them. We got a call once from an employee in jail that she would not be able to make her shift. She was in a car with a group of friends that got pulled over and did not know there was a warrant for her arrest for an unpaid court fine from years ago.

We did not judge her; we knew her heart, which was not her character. We bailed her out of jail and paid her fine. It was over $1,000, and she agreed to work it off, and she did—every cent of it. Do not be afraid to take a chance on people; everyone makes mistakes, and believing in people is always the right thing to do.

She worked for us for many years after this incident and became one of our assistant directors.

Have a great relationship with your people so they won't be afraid to ask for help if they get into trouble.

Remember this important Secret on Corporate Leadership: ***Be a positive (neutral) role model at all times.***

Secret #33

Be Careful of Micromanaging Your Team

A micro-manager is a boss who hovers over a subordinate assigned a project when they are trying to complete the job, usually offering advice to this person to help them complete the project the way they want it done. This typically drives the subordinate crazy, conveys mistrust for the way they were doing it, and makes this person not want to do another thing to help the boss in the future.

In previous Secrets, we learned the importance of delegating. We also learned about the importance of good leadership. As a leader, you will have to delegate tasks to others; it is your responsibility. Trust is the critical component of leadership for the employee to do the job without feeling like they are under a microscope.

The perfectionist control freak owner will have the most challenging time not micromanaging. If this is you, it is time to knock that chip off your shoulder because part of you thinks you are better than others.

Why would you not trust someone else? Can you do it better? WRONG. You can do it better "in your eyes," but that is not always the case.

Once Brian trusted others to help with projects, he never felt so liberated. Trust is a powerful leadership skill. Mentorship is another good leadership skill. Mentor your team so they know how a project should be done and trust them to do it their way. It may not be the exact way you would do it, but it is likely good enough and allows you time to do more important things.

Your team members will thank you for trusting them with this huge responsibility. When you have extra time in your life and your team is working well without you hovering over them, you will thank us for helping with this area of your business.

Remember this important Secret on Corporate Leadership: ***Be careful of micromanaging your team.***

Chapter 3 Notes

_____
_____
_____
_____
_____
_____
_____
_____
_____
_____
_____
_____
_____
_____
_____
_____
_____
_____
_____
_____
_____

Chapter 4

Dynasty Culture

"I look for two things when I hire a new employee: ambition and humility. Without a proven track record of initiative and ambition, it's likely the person becomes a drain rather than a contributor to the company, even the really smart, talented ones."
~ Justin McLeod

Fifty years ago when someone got out of college and got a job, they would expect to be doing that job for 40 years and then retire. That trend started shifting in the late 1900s, and a person today can expect to work 8-10 jobs in their lifetime, probably more.

No more are the days when a worker was loyal to the company that gave them a start. Today's employees want more and more, and unfortunately, with taxes, fees, expenses, and regulations going through the roof, there is less and less profit to pay more and more payroll expenses.

Workplace culture is vital to creating a sustainable business, and if you wish to build a dynasty, you need to create a fantastic dynasty culture. You need a workplace where team members feel appreciated, loved, cared for, and admired. One where they feel the value of their work and feel like they are making a difference in the world.

In this chapter, we will discuss how to improve your culture. Be sure to check out our YouTube videos for more ideas on how to improve your staff culture in the future.

Secret #34

Know Your Teacher Turnover Rate

Teacher turnover is expensive. Not only does it cost financially, it also costs dearly in lost institutional knowledge. It is reported that it costs over $3,000 to replace an experienced teacher that has left your company. If you have 10-15 teachers go a year, you can see how that can impact the bottom line and your institutional experience.

The less experienced your team is, the greater the chance that mistakes can happen. Mistakes are costly as well. Children could be injured or worse. Licensing violations will be multiplied the more inexperienced your team has as well.

It is best to keep who you have, so we will give you tips on this and the following few Secrets to help keep your current team of experienced teachers right where they are on your payroll!

First, you have to have a teacher retention plan. What is your goal? Do you have one? What was your teacher turnover last year? Most center owners do not know the answer to that question. You cannot fix what you don't know is broken; if you do not see how bad your retention system is, you have no idea when and how to fix it.

Let's calculate your teacher turnover. Take the number of employees who began the year but were no longer with your company at year's end and divide it by the total number of W2s you printed on December 31. Let's use 50 employees who left the company and 100 W2's printed.

$$50/100 = .50$$

multiply .50 by 100 = 50% turnover

Let's do another example. Ten employees left the company, and 50 W2s were printed.

$$10/50 = .2$$

$$.2 \text{ times } 100 = 20\% \text{ turnover}$$

Now let's calculate yours:
December 31, 20_____

\# Employees who quit during the year: _____ (a)

\# of W2's printed on the above date: _____ (b)

(a)_____ / (b)_____ = _____
x 100 = _____% turnover

Another way to calculate how many employees left during the year is to take the number of W2s and Subtract the total number of employees on the payroll on December 31st.

Now that we know our number, we can get a plan to improve the number. Each year we should strive to lower that number; by doing so, we save much money and make our center safer and a much better place to work.

Most child care centers have turnover in the 35-40% range each year. You are doing well if you can get your number below 30%. If you have it below 20%, you are in the top few centers worldwide and likely have a great workplace culture. Keep striving to get that number lower and lower each year.

Remember this important Secret on Dynasty Culture: ***Know your teacher turnover rate.***

Secret #35

Create an Amazing Place to Work

Would you want to go to work for yourself? If you weren't an owner and wanted to get a job working at a child care center, would you pick your center or someone else's? Why? What makes yours so unique? Are you biased, or do you truly feel that way?

These are tough questions to ask. We have had dozens of teachers leave us over the years only to return months or years later. Why? Our culture was better than any center; they had to find that out for themselves.

We have had teachers leave us for $3.00 an hour more working elsewhere only to return to their job a month later, realizing that happiness is much more than a paycheck.

Money cannot buy long-term happiness; you cannot buy your employee's loyalty. We found out that paying our staff more did not do too much to move the turnover needle; offering bonuses, employee recognition, and having a fun workplace to work in did far more.

What are your center's core values? Is fun one of them? Is your director a fun person to work for, or are they dull? Our directors are young, energetic, fun, passionate, and hard-working. They are the most complex working person in the building and are incredible leaders. They have great respect for all of their team members, which is why the team members are so loyal to them.

Having a director with excellent leadership makes all of the difference. It goes a long way if the director does a great job recognizing the staff members and showing great appreciation. People want to work where they feel valued and their work makes a difference. Do your employees feel this way?

There are many ways you can show recognition to your team members. We recommend the book *Relationship Roadmap: Real World Strategies for Building a Positive, Collaborative Culture in Your Preschool* by Sindye

Alexander. This book has hundreds of ideas on improving the relationship with your team members to lower staff turnover.

Book Recommendation:
Relationship Roadmap
by Sindye Alexander

Remember this important Secret on Dynasty Culture: ***Create an amazing place to work.***

Secret #36

Recognize Employees for Their Hard Work

Everyone loves to be recognized, and it does not have to be elaborate or expensive to have an impact. Sometimes it's the little things that have the most significant impact.

Child care is sometimes a fast-paced and chaotic environment. Well, most of the time, it is. Okay, all of the time! A good director and teacher are constantly on the go, and only a naptime when all of the children sleep allows for a breather, but sometimes that does not even happen.

It is easy for an owner or director to forget to say "thank you" to the hard-working members of your staff. Some of you may be thinking, why should I thank them for doing their job? Most teachers do above and beyond what their job description calls for, which is the part that needs thanks.

I have never met a teacher that does not use their own money to buy stuff for their "kids." Any good teacher loves the children they care for like they were their own.

When we onboard new employees, we ask them for personal information that allows us to get to know them better, and it enables us to tailor recognition to precisely what the person desires. There is a big difference between recognition and personalized recognition.

The reason we personalize our recognition system is this. Imagine you were to get everyone at your center a coffee shop gift card. You would tell yourself; I am such a great owner getting everyone a gift to show my appreciation. But the one staff member that hates coffee feels unappreciated and left out. Your noble intention backfired.

That is why personalized recognition is so important. Reward people based on their likes and dislikes, and they will love you so much for taking the time to know them.

A $5 gift card to their favorite coffee shop does more positive good for an employee than a $25 card to a place they do not like. It's not the amount; it's the amount of caring that goes into the gesture.

Remember this important Secret on Dynasty Culture: *Recognize employees for their hard work.*

Secret #37

Keep it Small While Making it Big

While building your dynasty, one of the hardest things to do is keep your business small while making it big. What we mean by this is having each center feel like they are the brand and a critical piece of the entire operation.

In our business, each center director feels essential because they are important. We don't burden them with focusing on company financial goals; we want them to focus on their own center's goals. It is up to us to worry about the business as a whole.

Allowing the directors to focus on their center keeps the business small and allows the owner to build the business as big as they wish.

By keeping it small, the team members feel more like a family. Each family consists of parents and children. But parents are part of a more prominent family. When you look at your immediate family, you tend not to focus on being a part of an even bigger family.

Once or twice a year, we get the whole family together, similar to a family reunion you might go to with your extended family. We force our team members to sit with those from our other centers and get them out of their comfort zone to learn from their peers. At the end of each meeting, we always come back to each center gathering for a short staff meeting. This brings the whole team back together and unites the family again.

It will take some getting used to, but in the long run, if you can keep your business small in the eyes of the team while making it as big as you desire, you will have a hardworking workforce that always feels like they are part of a family. These teachers will have better overall retention and will be much happier at their jobs.

Remember this important Secret on Dynasty Culture: ***Keep it small while making it big.***

Secret #38

Pay Your Employees Well

Building a child care dynasty may be the goal, but you should not do it by paying your employees less than the market rate for their hard work. When we started, we paid our employees what we could because we were barely making ends meet ourselves.

As we grew, we started offering better pay and more benefits, all while being able to preserve capital for expansion. It was a fine line to walk to ensure that as the business continued to grow, we could offer more and more to our staff to help us get to that place.

We have seen many times that a business overpays employees too much upon opening. Most of the time, a former teacher opens the school, and out of guilt and lack of business knowledge thinks she will be different from the competitors and pays her staff well above average. I commend this person, but when a recession hits, and it will (averages once every ten years), this person will be out of business, and the employees will be out of a job.

Our business survived two recessions without laying off a single teacher because we pay slightly better than the market rate, and we have kept a healthy savings account in reserve for a rainy day when revenues drop. During a recession, enrollment (and revenues) can drop by up to 30%.

We have witnessed dozens of owners who had to close their doors within one or two years who overpaid employees on day one. When starting the business, there are unforeseen expenses that an owner does not think of, and once you establish pay with your staff, it is hard to revise it downwards.

As your business grows and you have less and less debt and plenty of savings, you can and must invest in your team members by increasing pay and benefits. This way, the business is in zero danger of failing and will have secure jobs for a long time.

Suppose you insist on paying more early, before you can afford it. In that case, we recommend only paying the market rate in their hourly wage but giving a performance or profit-sharing bonuses. This way, when a recession hits or revenue is down, you are not stuck paying high salaries, which could sink the company and force all teachers to the unemployment line.

There are plenty of benefits you can offer that cost the company zero. There are supplemental health, dental, life, and disability policies that employees can have access to through your company. You can set many of these up pre-tax as a payroll deduction. Two companies we have used in the past are Aflac and Allstate Benefits. Both are very good and will give your employees some protection if your center cannot afford to offer a full health insurance package.

A SIMPLE IRA is also a benefit you can offer that does not cost a lot to administer. You will match your employee's pre-tax contributions, and they will be invested in the stock market in securities of the employee's choosing. Contact a securities broker in your area, and they will be able to set this up for you. As the owner, you can participate in this IRA and have the company match your deductions. We recommend contributing the maximum amount allowed by law to get the best tax advantages.

Child care discounts are another excellent benefit you can offer for employees. The discount can be based on how many years the employee has been working. Many of our past clients provided 25% discount for under a year service and 50% for over one year. We have seen free childcare for employees with over three years of service and directors. Be careful about offering free childcare to all employees; this can be costly and mess up your ratios. As the owner, find a number you are comfortable with that attracts quality teachers with children to work for you while rewarding teachers for longevity with your company.

Some centers offer free food to staff members. The USDA allows the food prepared for the children to be served to staff members who sit and eat with the children. This saves the staff member money from eating out each day for lunch, and USDA meals are very healthy.

In summary, pay your employees the best you can but always think long-term and have at least six months of payroll savings for the next recession. This way, you will be the one center standing as your competitors start dropping, and then you can hire their staff and enroll their children.

Remember this important Secret on Dynasty Culture: ***Pay your employees well.***

Secret #39

Have an Amazing Onboarding Routine

First impressions are lasting impressions. When onboarding a new employee, you have one chance to affirm their decision to join your team, and that is the first day and the first week.

Have you ever bought something, and buyer's remorse set in within a day or two? That can happen to your new employee if you give them the impression in the first week that they are just another body to change diapers and not a special part of a team making a massive difference in the world.

To have an amazing onboarding experience, plan the first day to be an extraordinary day. As the owner, you need to invest in your onboarding routine, which will pay handsome dividends over time by reducing teacher turnover.

Some ideas on the teacher's first day are a welcoming message in the lobby welcoming them to the team, flowers, a personalized card, a gift bag, and a card signed by all staff members. We highly recommend giving all new team members a copy of *Child Care Mindset: 30 Days of Growth and Transformation* (this is the book we wrote for teachers, it makes a life-changing onboarding gift). During the first week, please encourage them to read this book during naptime; it will help their mindset and reduce teacher turnover over time.

The owner (or the director if the owner does not work in the center) should buy lunch for the new team member and eat with them on day one, getting to know them. Nothing builds camaraderie like breaking bread together. When this teacher was growing up, their family likely ate together. This simple act will instantly make this new team member feel like part of your family. One good thing about buying lunch for them on day one is they can't go to lunch and not return!

On day one, the new teachers should be assigned a mentor. This mentor will be someone the new employee can contact anytime they have questions. This mentor has to be someone that is trusted to be a positive role model. One idea is to bonus a mentor for everyone that stays six months or more; she will get a bonus, which gives her an incentive to help this person stay with the company.

During the entire first week, check in each day with your new team member. A personalized card on days three and five is also a good idea and makes them feel appreciated. After that, a card and check-in every 30 days for the first six months is also vital. They always have to feel you care about them and are a valued team member.

If you do not wear name tags, be sure to get them a stick-on one to wear on week one so that everyone can learn the new person's name. A person's name is the sweetest sound to them, so having everyone know their name is significant.

Be sure to properly train them and not just stick them in a classroom by themselves with screaming kids in their first hour. That is a surefire way to have them quit within the first few days. Before setting them free, it is worth the extra time to ensure they are comfortable with your policies.

An excellent onboarding procedure is a key to reducing employee turnover and making employees happier. If new people are so glad and perform well early on, it takes the burden off seasoned staff who do not have to pick up the slack.

Remember this important Secret on Dynasty Culture: ***Have an amazing onboarding routine.***

Secret #40

Use Core Values to Hire, Reward, Discipline, and Terminate

You have spent time creating your company's core values; good for you! Now, what do you do with them? You use them to your advantage to make better employees.

Hiring: In your advertisements for new team members, you need to list the company's core values and let prospective employees know that they will be required to live up to the company's core values as part of their job description.

During the interview, the person doing the interview needs to ask the person they are interviewing how they interpret each core value and whether they can perform the job while living within the core value.

For example, one of our core values is Family: *"We treat your child as if they were our very own."* We will ask the prospective employee if they can give enough love and attention to each child and treat them like they were her own. An affirmative answer tells you that they will be able to live up to that core value, then you repeat it with all of your core values.

Rewarding: When we walk around our center, we look to catch teachers doing something right. Unfortunately, many owners and directors look for what employees are doing wrong. We are always looking for someone who is setting a great example and living up to our core values, and we will publicly reward them or give them public praise on our social media page.

Other employees see the positive attention living up to the core values brings and the productivity of all staff members increases. Everyone loves praise, so use it often and watch as your staff works overtime at living the company's core values.

Disciplining: When you are a team member not living up to your core values, you must address it quickly and write which core value they are not living up to. Documentation is essential and can help you avoid problems later on. There always has to be a written consequence of repeated behavior, so they know what happens if it is not corrected quickly.

Termination: If disciplining does not correct the problem, you can terminate the employee for not living up to the company's values. In the termination write-up, state the violated core value and why it is grounds for dismissal.

Using the standard of core values to hire, reward, discipline, and terminate, allows you to have a standard to hold employees accountable. It will make the owner or director's job so much easier and help the team members know the rules to live by. The best part is that the employees are the ones who made these rules that they will be held accountable for.

Remember this important Secret on Dynasty Culture: ***Use core values to hire, reward, discipline, and terminate.***

Secret #41

Quickly Terminate Negative Employees

What is the quickest way to have an entirely negative workforce? Let a super-negative employee stay on your payroll long enough to infect everyone else.

Negative employees are like cancer; it is unwelcome and can spread quickly. It spreads without the director or owner noticing until it is too late. A toxic workplace is tough to turn around, so avoid it at all costs.

A toxic mindset is hard to overcome, so remediation does not often work. Telling employees with a toxic mindset that their negative attitude is not welcomed will fall on deaf ears because they think their attitude is fine. It is everyone else who has the problem.

As the owner or director, it is essential to check the mindset temperature of your center often. Knowing your team's baseline attitude is vital, so when you see changes happening, you need to quickly investigate and find the source of the toxicity and cut it out.

Doing so will help you save the attitude of the center. Wait too long and you will have serious problems that you will not be able to recover from without replacing everyone, which is very hard to do.

In our experience, the employees who have been with us the longest, mostly over ten years, is where the attitude starts to shift to one of a toxic mindset. It may be burnout or frustration with getting older and still doing the same job that takes a toll over time. Be sure to check in on employees that have been doing the same position for over ten years; they are the most susceptible to a feeling of resentment for younger staff members whose starting pay is so much higher than theirs was, and in their opinion, they don't deserve it.

Book Recommendation:
Get Out
by Vernon Mason, Jr.

Someone who has been with you a long time is hard to let go. We have had to do it several times. You are doing this person a favor. Each person we have had to do this with landed on their feet and was much happier leaving the industry. We tell our employees that when they stop loving the kids and making a difference in the world, it becomes just a job, and it is time to move on.

Remember this important Secret on Dynasty Culture: ***Quickly terminate negative employees.***

Secret #42

Have a Careers Page on your Website

Your website is your company billboard that is functioning 24/7/365. Most owners spend money on their website to attract customers but only recently have owners gotten serious about attracting new employees on the company website.

A well-thought-out careers page is vital to a growing child care center. Since you will likely be hiring continually, it is essential to have a place where prospective employees can find out information about your school.

Your careers page should include the following information:
- Company Core Values
- Employee video and written testimonials
- Pictures of team members smiling
- Job description
- Link to apply online
- Pay range (depending on experience)
- Benefits
- Qualifications needed
- Open positions
- Equal opportunity employer statement

Be sure to include heart-centered statements like: "Make a difference in the life of a child," "Work in a career so rewarding that we hate to call it to work," or "Make an impact on a caring team." You want to tug on their emotional heartstrings.

More than likely, where they are currently working, they are not making a difference in the world, which is why they are looking into the child care field. No one gets into child care for compensation; they want to make a difference. Showing them in your advertisements will get them to act much more quickly.

Having an online application is smart because they can quickly apply while you have them emotionally. Be sure to reach out to them as soon as possible after they fill out the application; the quicker, the better while their emotions are the highest.

We wish you the best in your search for employees that want to make a difference in the world. They are out there; you just have to find them and create a fantastic experience for them once you hire them. Doing so will help change the world, one child at a time.

Remember this important Secret on Dynasty Culture: *Have a careers page on your website.*

Chapter 4 Notes

_____
_____
_____
_____
_____
_____
_____
_____
_____
_____
_____
_____
_____
_____
_____
_____
_____
_____
_____
_____
_____
_____
_____
_____
_____
_____
_____

Chapter 5

Advanced HR and Legal

"I am convinced that nothing we do is more important than hiring and developing people. At the end of the day, you bet on people, not on strategies."
~ Lawrence Bossidy

We are now in probably the most boring part of the book, advanced HR and legal. It is the part of the book that, if not done right, can cost you dearly.

Pay close attention to the following Secrets, and please do not skip over this chapter. Take good notes and make sure you shore up your policies to ensure federal and state compliance. Doing so will help you not only sleep better at night but also have less stress while at work.

Secret #43

Have an Attorney Review all Documents

In today's litigious society, someone will sue you for looking at them the wrong way. We have been sued before, and most successful business owners have. The Secret is to have iron-clad documentation that holds up in a court of law.

Your corporate attorney should review every single document a parent or employee signs. This person will ensure that the company (and you) are protected should you get sued.

It is not a bad idea to have your website reviewed as well. Anything that a potential employee or customer sees and can interpret one way or another should be reviewed to ensure it passes legal muster.

Having an attorney on retainer is also a good idea. A retainer is an amount the attorney keeps as a credit on your account should you need their services in the future.

Don't be a cheapskate here; spend the money to have a professional review your information. A lawsuit can bankrupt you and put you out of business.

Remember this important Secret on Advanced HR and Legal: *Have an attorney review all documents.*

Secret #44

Read and Know the Americans
With Disabilities Act

Have you ever heard the old saying, "what you don't know won't hurt you"? In this case, what you don't know can hurt you. The Americans With Disabilities Act (ADA) was an attempt to help disabled people have an even shot at the workforce without fear of discrimination. It was signed in 1990 by President George H.W. Bush.

Over the years, many types of disabilities were added to the ADA list, and most recently, Long Covid was advised as a qualifier under ADA. Long Covid is a long-term ailment that lingers for years after someone has had Covid. Most owners have no idea that type of ailment is protected.

As an owner, you need to read the ADA and know it inside and out. Whoever does the hiring needs to know it as well. Is your center ADA compliant? You may say your center is grandfathered, and it may be for local ordinances, but more than likely not for ADA.

We had someone apply once that was in a wheelchair. She was more than qualified, so we hired her to be a great fit. She could not work alone due to safety concerns, but she was the head teacher who had an assistant. She was with us for over a year and left on her own. We would hire someone else like this with no hesitation.

We also hired a deaf teacher, and she was fantastic as well. We had to have an assistant for her as well, but we were able to make that accommodation. We also hired a teacher with Down's Syndrome; she was like a big kid and had so much fun daily with the kids. She was a Special Olympian and a great person.

Brian has been disabled his whole life. Born with Osteogenesis Imperfecta, often referred to as brittle bone disease, he never let it stop him from doing amazing things in life. This is why we hire people with disabilities. Everyone deserves a chance. If you want to make a difference in a child's life, we want to ensure we do our best to accommodate you should you have a disability.

Read the ADA and know it inside and out, but don't be afraid to take a chance. You may be pleasantly surprised that this person will likely be very loyal and work extra hard to prove themselves.

Remember this important Secret on Advanced HR and Legal: ***Read and know the Americans with Disabilities Act.***

Secret #45

Be Aware of Protected Employee Classes

Terminating someone from a protected class is a little trickier than someone who is not in a protected class. The key is documentation which we will learn about in Secret #46. (Be sure to check to see if your state has additional protected classes).

Federally protected classes include:

- Race
- Color
- Religion or creed
- National origin or ancestry
- Sex (including gender, pregnancy, sexual orientation, or gender identity)
- Physical or mental disability
- Age
- Veteran status
- Genetic information (including family medical history)
- Citizenship

When terminating employment for someone on the list above, you have to ensure that you have ironclad paperwork backing you up so in case you get sued, your case will hold up in court. Even if you are in an at-will state, you can still have issues with protected class termination.

Always have Employment Practices Liability Insurance to protect you from lawsuits from an employee in a protected class. Since the average judgment and legal fees are over $400,000, this insurance will protect your business from a potentially fatal hit.

Remember this important Secret on Advanced HR and Legal: ***Be aware of protected employee classes.***

Secret #46

Document, Document, Document

You will never have to worry when terminating someone if you have a policy that everything is fully documented at all times. Any disciplinary action, however slight, gets documented.

You need to have a written employee warning system that documents the steps you will take if an employee is not performing. They will need a chance to correct the deficiencies, and a corrective action plan should be discussed.

Be sure to have your attorney review your disciplinary and termination procedures to ensure they can pass legal muster should you get sued by someone who gets terminated.

Before you are going to terminate someone from a protected class, be sure to show the documentation to your attorney and make sure that everything is ironclad.

You will notice a pattern here; protect yourself! A little preventive legal expense will save you many legal headaches later. Documentation is the key to a good night's sleep!

Remember this important Secret on Advanced HR and Legal: *Document, document, document.*

Secret #47

Have a Detailed Operations Manual

If you are in expansion mode, you may add centers by starting organically or purchasing a center. More than likely you will be dealing with new staff who are not experienced with your company policies.

An operations manual allows you to expand quicker by bringing new staff up to speed faster. This manual covers every possible scenario that could happen at your schools and the policy. An operations manual is NEVER finished; it is constantly evolving and changing. It must be accessible to every company member, but only certain people will be given editing rights.

The best way to start an operations manual is to start writing. As things happen in your business, write a policy. Kid gets stung by a bee and has an allergic reaction, write a policy. If a teacher has a seizure on the playground, write a policy. For the teacher who wants to paint her classroom, create a policy. Supplies need to be ordered by the Director, be sure there is a policy.

A standardized operations manual that is the same for all centers in an organization is key to scaling a prominent child care center dynasty. Each center will be held to the same standards, and all employees will have access to know what the rules are. This level of transparency will build trust within your organization and make things run smoothly.

Remember this important Secret on Advanced HR and Legal: *Have a detailed operations manual.*

Secret #48

Consider Outsourcing Human Resources

The use of technology has made it much easier for a center owner to do business. In our early days, we used paper ledgers to track our tuition collected; now, everything is revolutionized with apps and software specific to our industry.

Human resources are one area where you can hire someone in-house to handle the paperwork and legal aspects of having employees. This can get expensive for a small company to have a dedicated person handling human resources matters.

A few years ago, outsourced HR companies started popping up; now there are a lot of them. They will help you with the legal requirements of having employees in your state and take care of paperwork should you have to terminate an employee.

We highly recommend outsourcing HR if you have less than 150 employees. You will save significantly and be well protected from a liability perspective. We will not recommend one company over another here, do your research and find which company is best for your particular needs.

Remember this important Secret on Advanced HR and Legal: *Consider outsourcing human resources.*

Chapter 5 Notes

Chapter 6

Dynasty Financial Strategies

"Focus on solving real problems and not on making money. There will be enough takers for your solutions. You will help make lives of some people better, and money will follow."
~ Bhavish Aggarwal

The key to building a child care dynasty is a firm financial foundation. Expansion normally takes capital, and if you borrow money, the lending institution will need to see you have sound financial footing before they lend to you.

If you follow the Secrets we outline in the next few pages; you will put yourself on solid financial grounds to help prepare you for expanding your dynasty.

You must have a plan that may take years to develop fully. Be patient, and do not get yourself in financial trouble to reach some arbitrary goal. It is far better to miss a goal and be in good financial shape than to hit a goal and be strapped financially.

Secret #49

Pay the Least Amount of Tax
Required by Law

We have not met one person that enjoys paying taxes; we sure don't. It is a necessary evil, but there are ways you can lower your tax burden, and we will go over some of them here.

1. **Keep good records:** If you were to get audited and you cannot produce receipts or invoices, you will lose the deduction, and it will cost you money. It pays to keep good records.

2. **Are you an S-Corporation?** If so, keep your salary as low as your CPA is comfortable and take the rest of the net profits as distributions or dividends. This will save you over 15% in taxes by avoiding Social Security taxes on both the employee and the employer.

3. **Track your business mileage:** Many apps will track the mileage you drive for business. If your office is in your home, you can deduct trips to and from your schools to deliver supplies, food, etc. Keeping track of every mile will put a significant amount of money back in your pocket instead of the tax man's.

4. **Company car purchase:** As of publishing, the IRS allows you to purchase a vehicle weighing over 6000 pounds (Full-size SUV) and get a 100% write-off in year one (accelerated depreciation), even if you finance the car. It is a great way to reduce your tax burden and get new wheels. We have done this twice. Just a reminder that if you do this, you won't be able to claim mileage on this vehicle, but you can claim all gas, oil, insurance, and maintenance.

5. **Invest in real estate:** Buying residential or commercial real estate as an investment will yield incredible tax savings to offset some of your child care earnings. We will be discussing this in greater detail later in the book.

6. **Maximize retirement account contributions:** Depending on your income, certain retirement accounts will be available to you to get some tax-deferred benefits. Consult your financial advisor (and CPA) for ways to increase retirement savings while lowering your tax burden.

7. **Have a good CPA prepare your tax return.** Never do the taxes yourself or have someone that is not a Certified Public Accountant (CPA). These professionals are the highest trained in tax law and give you the most protection.

8. **Put your children to work:** Your children can get paid for helping in the business. They will have to report the income if it meets a certain threshold but will have zero or very low tax liability compared to you. Consult your CPA for the best strategy.

Disclaimer: We are not tax professionals. Be sure to consult your CPA on which tax strategy is right for your business.

Remember this important Secret on Dynasty Financial Strategies: ***Pay the least amount of tax required by law.***

Secret #50

Have an Emergency Financial Plan

A recession hits, and you lose 35% of your revenue; how long could you stay open? Your building floods, and you have to be closed for repairs for 45 days. Could you stay in business? Your furnace breaks, and it costs $25,000 to replace. Can you afford this without having to go into debt?

These are real-world possibilities that many owners have faced. We have been through two recessions, replaced two furnaces, and had two different directors quit on the same day, and we came through much more potent than before. How did we do it? We had a financial plan.

Many center owners run their businesses like they run their personal lives, living paycheck to paycheck. You risk your entire business if you have less than six months of business and personal expenses in a savings account.

When your business is doing well, start putting money each month in a company and a personal savings account as much as possible. Have it come out automatically, and be disciplined not to touch it. Put it in these accounts when you have extra money and watch them grow. Let's examine how much you will need to protect your business and personal life.

Look at your tax return from last year and find the total expenses of your business. You need 25% of that amount in a savings account (or an investment account) to prepare for a rainy day, which will come eventually.

Look at your total expenses in your household, and you will need 25% of that amount in a personal savings account. Once these two steps are done, you are ready to grow your dynasty.

Keep in mind that as your dynasty grows, the amount you need in savings grows too. You need this money to hedge against unforeseen circumstances that can put you out of business, mainly in an economic downturn.

Multi-center operators are particularly hit with recessions because very few have the emergency savings needed to weather an economic storm. Many of them do not survive a recession; we have seen it firsthand many times.

Recessions are incredible buying opportunities for owners that are in good financial condition. You will be able to get financing and pick up a struggling center for 25-50 cents on the dollar (or even less!). The secret is to have a financial plan and ensure that it includes having capital in reserve should a fantastic buying opportunity surface.

Remember this important Secret on Dynasty Financial Strategies: ***Have an emergency financial plan.***

Secret #51

Create an Expansion Plan

If future expansion is in your short- or long-term plans, you must prepare a financial plan to meet that future demand. Do not wait until a center comes on the market to realize you do not have money for a down payment. You need to start preparing years before you put your expansion plan in order. Do not start saving for expansion until you have 6-12 months' worth of all expenses in a savings account.

If you plan on buying a building or an existing school, you will need a 10-25% down payment, depending on how you fund your expansion. Take the average center price and multiply it by 25%; that is a good rule of thumb for what you should have saved for a down payment. Even if a company will fund 90%, it is suitable only to borrow 75% to keep debt payments lower.

If you plan on starting a school from scratch and leasing, you will need about a year of lease payments, six months of payroll, marketing dollars, and money for equipment in the bank before signing the lease. If you do, try only to borrow 75% of the money to have more skin in the game. It is far better not to have to borrow anything if you are not buying the building. It will put you in a better financial position.

It may take a year or two to save the money needed, but that is okay. You don't want to open more than one center a year anyway. We have done two centers in one year, and it is challenging. Patience is the key when it comes to finding the right deal. Do not rush into something you will regret later.

Remember this important Secret on Dynasty Financial Strategies: ***Create an expansion plan.***

Secret #52

Have a Handle on Cash Flow

The larger your school gets, the more cash flow will swing. You have to have a firm handle on this, or you will get into trouble. We recommend keeping at least a month's worth of expenses in your checking account to handle the swings in cash flow.

The reason cash flow swings is that tuition is not always constant. You may collect parent payments regularly, but how about state and federal subsidy payments? These can be late and not on schedule, which can cause some issues with heavily subsidized centers.

If you pay your credit card bill in full monthly, as we do, you can have a substantial payment coming out once a month. If you pay your employees bi-weekly, like most centers, you will have two large monthly withdrawals (and three a few times a year). You will also have vendor payments coming out at varying times each month.

Not all of the money in your checking account is yours. It belongs to vendors, the IRS, employees, mortgage companies or landlords, and utility companies, and then a small percentage is yours. It differs from your checking account, which is mostly your money.

We keep a cash journal and track the daily balances of our accounts. It is a simple spreadsheet that lists the charges and the daily balances and then totals them. We track these totals and always know what our average daily balance is. We never let the daily balance fall below twice our average payroll amount. We also have a hefty savings account, and our bank would automatically pull out of our savings account if our checking account balance were short. Always make sure you set up auto-transfers, just in case. You never want to bounce a check to an employee; that would be very bad!

Know your cash flow, and only pull out the cash you know you won't need for future expenses. Doing it this way will protect you and the company from financial problems down the road.

Remember this important Secret on Dynasty Financial Strategies: ***Have a handle on cash flow.***

Secret #53

Contribute the Maximum Allowed to a Company Retirement Plan

Offering an employee retirement plan is an excellent way to provide a great employee benefit that does not cost the company much money but gives them and you a great way to save money on taxes and save for retirement in the process.

You can use several different plans, so we recommend contacting an investment advisor to discuss what is best for your company. Be sure to do your research and make sure that the fees are reasonable.

The most significant benefit of having a company retirement plan is that you can contribute the maximum allowable by law. We highly recommend that you invest the maximum amount yearly, which will considerably lower your taxes. You will be required to provide a partial match to your employee plans, which will be tax-deductible to the company (you can even match your contributions).

Be sure never to touch this money because significant financial penalties and taxes will be due. Let this money grow until retirement, and you will benefit from compound interest.

Remember this important Secret on Dynasty Financial Strategies: ***Contribute the maximum allowed to a company retirement plan.***

Secret #54

Have an Investment Strategy
to Build Wealth

Besides having a company retirement plan and contributing the maximum, you need an investment strategy to build wealth. As we discussed earlier, your priority is to build savings for a rainy day. Your second priority is to fund a retirement account to maximize tax savings fully. The third priority is to develop an investment plan or long-term wealth building.

Some people choose to invest in the stock market, and we will not say anything wrong about that. In the last Secret, we told you to invest the maximum in a company retirement plan, which is the stock market.

We chose to invest in real estate because, over time, it has done better than the stock market, and the tax code is written to favor real estate investors. While you are building wealth in real estate, the government is giving you incredible write-offs, and if something happens to you, it can be easily transferred to your heir tax-free.

Your first real estate purchases should be the child care center buildings you operate out of. We initially did not own our real estate; we slowly acquired it over time. Be patient and look for deals; do not overpay! Never be in a hurry to acquire. Every time we were patient we were rewarded with a much better price.

As of the writing of this publication, we currently own 27 residential units and six commercial units. Ten years ago we held nothing. This shows you how fast you can grow with an investment plan. If you want us to help you put an investment plan together, please email us at info@childcaregenius.com. This is what we specialize in!

Remember this important Secret on Dynasty Financial Strategies: *Have an investment strategy to build wealth.*

Secret #55

Have a Top-Notch CPA; not a Bookkeeper, do Your Taxes

Many times in this book, you will see where we recommend money-saving tips; doing your taxes will not be one of them. You need to pay handsomely to have the best possible CPA do your taxes. This is one area you do not want to skimp on.

A Certified Public Accountant (CPA) is a licensed professional with specific education and continuing education to stay licensed.

You want an aggressive CPA that will go after every possible deduction and have you paying the least amount of taxes possible. The tax savings alone will more than pay for the extra amount of paying a CPA vs. an accountant or bookkeeper.

Make sure you find someone that is experienced in doing child care taxes. We have a unique profession that can be a high risk for an audit because a lot of clients pay cash, which is usually a red flag for the IRS. A CPA with child care tax experience can avoid a lengthy IRS audit headache.

We have been using the same CPA for 24 years, and he knows child care taxes inside and out. Establish a relationship where you speak monthly and never do any business expansion without involving your CPA in the discussions.

Remember this important Secret on Dynasty Financial Strategies: ***Have a top-notch CPA; not a bookkeeper, do your taxes.***

Secret #56

Have a Rewards Credit Card

There is a way to pay negative interest on a credit card. What is negative interest? When the credit card companies pay you to use their credit card! We have made hundreds of thousands of dollars from our credit card company, and we love doing it!

We love to travel, and airline credit cards are some of the most rewarding financially. We use the American Airlines credit card and the United Airlines credit card.

We get 1 mile for every dollar we spend, and it takes as little as 6,000 miles to get a free domestic airline ticket. So for spending $6,000 on things you would typically buy, you can get a $500 airline ticket for free; that is an excellent return on investment (that is an 8.33% ROI!)

We have traveled all over the world first class for free thanks to doing this, and have paid ZERO in credit card interest. Just pay off your entire balance monthly (set up on autopay to pay your full balance every month). If you do not pay off your monthly balance, it negates the value of the rewards they offer.

There are other reward cards out there. If you do not like to travel, find a card that pays you to use it, and you will get a good deal. We hope to see you on the beach somewhere you have traveled for free!

Remember this important Secret on Dynasty Financial Strategies: ***Have a rewards credit card.***

Secret #57

Live Humbly

We lived in the same house, raising our five children from the time we started building our child care business until we were multi-millionaires. We kept our standard of living low, kept investing in real estate and our future, and did not increase our lifestyle as our business grew. When we were completely debt free and had enough money to pay cash for a house, we upgraded to our lakefront dream home where we now live mortgage free.

As your income grows, you must be careful not to increase your lifestyle proportion to the growth. That is very dangerous. It is far better to reduce debt with the extra money and increase savings than to buy a newer car or a bigger house. There will be time for that later when you have 6-12 months of business expenses in the bank and a very low debt load. Save your money, and when you can pay cash for a new vehicle, you can afford to upgrade.

A good rule of thumb is to increase your lifestyle by no more than 20% of your previous year's income. For example, if you usually make $50,000 a year and this past year you made $60,000, do not go out and add $10,000 worth of annual spending to your budget; add no more than $2,000 to your yearly budget spending. Save the rest and pay down debt with it. Remember that what goes up can quickly come down, and eventually, it will. A recession will hit on average every 10-15 years, and when your income could decrease by 20-30% or more, will you still be able to pay your bills?

Living humbly is a surefire way to survive an economic downturn and be your center left standing when competitors go bankrupt.

Remember this important Secret on Dynasty Financial Strategies: *Live humbly.*

Secret #58

Avoid Staffing Hidden Blind Spots

New owners tend to get in trouble with this one. It is noble to want to pay your teachers more; after all, they are working so hard to care for the children. The problem is that a new owner does not consider all of the possible expenses you will incur when operating a child care center and gets in trouble by overextending.

One of the main reasons we see centers failing is by overpaying staff. Be sure to pay market rate or slightly above, but don't go crazy until you have a firm grip on your expenses. You will have a much better grasp of costs in year two than in year one.

If you get a grant to help with payroll, it is far better to offer bonuses than increasing salary. Salary increases are permanent (no one likes a pay cut), but bonuses are one-time money. Grants are one-time money, so be careful at committing long-term pay to a short-term funding source.

Overstaffing is another hidden blind spot, and the owner is often in the dark about its happening. Running a center is complicated, and sometimes teachers complain that they need help, and a director will hire extra people in the center to take the burden off the teachers, even when the owner cannot afford to do so.

You must hire teachers that can handle a classroom at the ratios allowed by law in your state. There is little profit in child care, and putting extra teachers in a school hits the bottom line pretty hard. We are not saying to avoid this totally; we are saying that you make sure you have a handle on proper staffing levels and approve everything above the minimum.

We have had directors who were horrible at knowing how to combine classrooms at the beginning and the end of the day to reduce overstaffing. This is very important to a center. Be sure that whoever handles your staffing knows how to move children around at the end of the day or during periods of staffing shortages to minimize payroll.

As the owner, you need to know your numbers, and tracking payroll costs as a percentage of revenue is vital. You not only need to know your number but need to follow it week to week, year to year. Look for irregularities that will signal an issue that needs to be corrected. Knowing your numbers is vital when building a child care dynasty.

Remember this important Secret on Dynasty Financial Strategies: *Avoid staffing hidden blind spots.*

Secret #59

Properly Manage Part-Time Care

In the last few years, we have seen part-time care grossly mismanaged by dozens of child care clients.

Most significant mistakes we have seen:

1. **Not surcharging for part-time care:** Part-time care is a premium and needs to be steeply surcharged.

2. **Not offsetting part-time care**: You want to ensure that your part-time children either offset other part-time children or are surcharged so heavily that you don't care if it offsets. You are relying on Monday-Wednesday-Friday and Tuesday-Thursday to offset. This does not work in most markets.

3. **Not allowing drop-in care**: Using drop-in care is a great way to increase revenue. Stipulations: You need to have them call in the morning to see if you have availability without having to bring in extra staff and if you do, they take that spot for a day. Charge a pretty penny, and it's all profit!

4. **Not having strict drop-off and pick-up times:** Be sure to have a period for drop-off and pick-up to protect the center. You don't want kids being dropped off at mealtime or nap time. Be strict with your times, and you will have happier directors.

Remember this important Secret on Dynasty Financial Strategies: **Properly manage part-time care.**

Secret #60

Beware of Over-Discounting Tuition

When we go to the store, we often see items discounted or marked down from their original price. Some people will go out of their way to look for these deals and save considerable money.

Child care is not one of those services people usually look for a deal on. Once in a while, someone may try to get a discount from you, that is not abnormal, but you need to establish early on what you can live with and never go below that number.

Each time you discount your services, you are cutting directly into bottom-line profits, which add up quickly. You cannot discount your payroll; your teachers would not like that. Vendors expect 100% payment as well. Would your landlord or mortgage company accept 90% of the rent or mortgage? NO! Since no one you pay will get anything less than full payment, every dime you offer as savings comes straight out of your pocket.

We recommend that if you want to offer a deal, do so with short-term discounts, not long-term ones. Offer a free registration fee or one or two free weeks. One-time savings instead of a certain amount off each week will add up to much money over the years the customer is with you.

Let's look at two examples:
1. The owner offers two weeks free at $200/week tuition.
2. The owner gives a $ 10-a-week discount.

Scenario 1 costs the owner $400; scenario 2 costs the owner $520...every year!

Never give long-term discounts; you will have a more stable bottom line as you build your business.

Remember this important Secret on Dynasty Financial Strategies: ***Beware of over-discounting tuition.***

Secret #61

Raise Tuition to Keep up with Market Forces

If you are charging less than the market rate for child care, you are hurting yourself and all of the centers in your area. The state will use market rate data to determine child care reimbursement rates, and when you keep your rates low, it keeps reimbursement rates low, which hurts you with future subsidized children.

Always be within 5% of the competitors in your area; do everything better than them. If you continue to follow the Child Care Genius Podcast™ and our training, you will be a step ahead of everyone else, and your center will be complete when they are struggling to get children.

Each year you need to raise your rates, and in some markets, you need to raise them twice annually to keep up with inflation. You are probably saying, "I can't do that to my parents; they will all leave me." We will show one Secret to raising rates they won't even notice.

We have a policy of raising our rates on January 1 of each year, and depending on how fast inflation is rising, we may also raise them on July 1. The January 1 increase is across the board and depends on market forces. It could be as little as $5 a week and as much as a 10% increase, depending on inflation and what other centers in my area are doing. This increase is for all existing customers.

Our July 1 increase is a hidden rate increase. We survey market data, and if another increase is warranted, we raise rates across the board for new families only. Doing this also raises the rates for existing families, but only when they have a birthday and get a rate adjustment.

For example: Let's say you have a 2 ½ year old that pays $250 a week for care (toddler rate), and normally the rate would decrease when the child turns 3 to $230 a week. You do a $ 10-a-week rate increase for new families only. When this toddler turns

3, they will pay $240 a week due to the $10-a-week increase on July 1. The parents never knew that rates increased.

Two things: In your handbook, put a statement that says tuition rates are subject to change at any time, with or without notice. Secondly, post the new tuition chart in your lobby on January 1 and July 1, so it is available for public display.

Not raising your tuition at least annually hurts your business and teachers. They deserve a pay raise; this increase is for them. When we raise our tuition in January, we tell our families that this tuition increase is going to the teachers who work so hard caring for the children, and we never get any pushback because of how we frame it.

Remember this important Secret on Dynasty Financial Strategies: ***Raise tuition to keep up with market forces.***

Secret #62

Keep Your Debt Load Low

There is smart debt, and there is not-so-smart debt. Low-interest secured debt that you borrow to buy a new location or to add a van or bus is smart debt. Getting a cash advance or taking a short-term high-interest-rate loan is not intelligent debt.

Work hard to keep your debt low, expenses low, savings high, and profits high. Doing this consistently over time will put you in an excellent position for future growth and allow you to dominate your market in a few years.

Never pay more than 3-4% over the prime rate when borrowing. NEVER pay credit card interest. If you charge items on a credit card, be sure to pay 100% of it off every single month! Paying credit card interest is NOT SMART! Don't do it!

We recommend having a home equity line of credit available to you in an emergency. The interest is tax deductible should you have to use it, and it is generally at a very low-interest rate. Over the years, we had to tap into our line of credit when state and federal funding was delayed, and it was quickly paid off.

Living well below your means and keeping your debts low is a great way to stay far ahead of the competition. When the next recession hits, and it will, you will be in an excellent position to buy out the competitor who is in financial trouble. It all starts with keeping your debt structure low.

Remember this important Secret on Dynasty Financial Strategies: ***Keep your debt load low.***

Secret #63

Recession is Coming - Be Ready!

Each time a recession hits, usually around every ten years or so, centers are forced to close, and dreams are shattered. Owners go bankrupt and have everything they have worked so hard for be lost forever.

Brian was one of the first child care coaches in the world to train on recession-proofing your child care business. Too often, we get caught up in the here and now that we lose focus and forget that history often repeats itself. If we know history, it gives us a HUGE competitive advantage.

While we would not wish for a recession on anyone, they are not very pleasant for many people; we are always prepared to expand our child care dynasty or our real estate empire when one happens.

Closely following the Secrets in this chapter will put you in a great financial position when the economy turns south. Keeping debts low and savings high will allow you to have a reduced income without sacrificing your lifestyle, and you will have enough to keep paying your employees even if you drop revenue sharply.

To be completely recession-proof, you need to do these four things:

1. **Be as debt free as possible**. Keeping obligations low will free up cash for other business areas, like savings and investments. Interest on debt is money that is not working for you.

2. **Have at least three months' worth of expenses in savings** (or stable liquid investment accounts). This includes ALL fees, payroll, rent, utilities, maintenance...everything! Doing this will make you strong competitively and help you survive the worst possible recession.

3. **Maintain your current centers at 90% or more occupancy** to maximize profit and use that profit to pay down debt and save. The old saying goes, "make hay while the sun shines."

4. **Have a recession expansion plan**. Have ten schools you are interested in buying in your head, and when things go south, be sure to contact them and try to buy them out before they go bankrupt. (It's harder to purchase assets when they are going through bankruptcy.) Later in the book, we will give you ideas on ways to contact them and what to say.

5. **Don't panic.** You may lose revenue, but you won't lose it all. You may have to dip into savings temporarily to cover costs; that is not a problem; that is what it is for. As centers around you close, you will be able to get their children and their staff, so all you have to do is wait them out. I once told my friend Joel when we were hiking in the woods. If we see a bear, I don't have to be able to outrun the bear; I only have to be able to outrun you. I was kidding, but you get my point. You have to survive longer than centers around you when times get tough.

Please do not think we are heartless about being prepared to increase market share when the proper situation arises. There are winners and losers in business; we choose to be on the winning side. It is a choice we make when we get up every day.

Real estate is another area where you can make a killing during a recession. Buying an investment property for investments or your child care center dynasty during a downturn is smart business. This is why a low debt structure is so important. You will be a good credit risk to a lender. They do not care as much about credit and revenue when you pay enough down payment. They only care about being able to recover their money should you default. Having a solid balance sheet makes you attractive to banks and mortgage companies.

We have bought three schools and several commercial and residential investment properties during recessions and got them all at great prices. Those properties are all producing income for us now that we have used to purchase a dozen more properties. Wealth makes more wealth if you do it properly. For us, it all started with a recession that we were prepared for.

Remember this important Secret on Dynasty Financial Strategies: ***Recession is coming - be ready!***

Secret #64

Create Generational Wealth

It is noble to want to leave some money for your children when you pass on; most people want to. Far too many people have nothing to leave because they did not save or they wasted their money when they were alive.

The principles we teach at *Child Care Genius University* will help you build generational wealth. Generational wealth is the ability to leave enough money to take care of several generations of your family.

Earlier in the book, we discussed buying real estate to diversify and add tax-advantaged growth to your portfolio. Real estate is one of the best ways to create generational wealth. You buy the property and pay off the mortgages before you die, and the rental income will pay your children's children over and over every month.

Be sure to set up a trust fund for the generational wealth that you will create. This fund will need to be managed and have stipulations; we recommend a clause that the properties cannot be sold and remain in the trust. The money from the trust can pay educational expenses, business start-up funds, first-time home down payment funds, or whatever you desire.

It is up to you how you want to set it up; think about how you would like them to spend the money. Do not just leave a lump sum; that would be irresponsible. This is money they did not work for, so it would not be treated the same as if it was performed for. Have strings attached to the funds for their benefit as well as yours? You will sleep better at night.

Your child care dynasty is also a great wealth builder. You can sell the business and keep the real estate, providing long-term rental income. You can sell everything and put the money into a trust for the next generation. There are many options. We discuss this more in-depth in Secret #94.

Remember this important Secret on Dynasty Financial Strategies: *Create generational wealth.*

Chapter 6 Notes

Chapter 7

Dynasty Marketing Strategy

"Marketing without data is like driving with your eyes closed."
~ Dan Zarrella

It takes money to make money; that is how the saying goes. You may be able to do a little bit of advertising on social media for free, but money needs to be spent to really make an impact.

The following five Secrets will give you marketing tips to help build your business. We have personally used each method we are sharing with you. You can do many other types of marketing, but we won't get into that today. The reason is that each area of the world is different regarding what marketing method works. For instance, in some states you can use billboards effectively, but in our state they are against the law so you won't see one. Newspapers are not read much any more as most people get their news online.

In some areas, weekly periodicals are a good choice for advertising. In others, you can put your ad on the side of a bus. As you can see, where to promote has a lot to do with where you live, so we will have to leave your local advertising dollars up to you.

The five Secrets below will help you no matter where you live; they are proven to be great marketing strategies you can use to get an incredible return on investment.

Secret #65

A Fully Functioning CRM System is a Must

CRM stands for Customer Relationship Management, a fancy customer database term. When we got our CRM system eight years ago, it was a complete game changer for our business.

Since then, our CRM system has made us millions of dollars by keeping our child center on the minds of our customers and working while we are sleeping to enroll more customers. A CRM system does not sleep, never needs a break, and does not forget. It keeps everything neat and organized and has one mission, to save you time and money.

Most directors are great at doing tours but notoriously bad at doing follow-ups. The CRM system will automate the follow-up work by continually "dripping" on a customer.

A "drip" campaign is something you can set up to keep sending pieces of information about your center every day for the first few days of contact when they are in the decision-making mode. By hitting them with messages, you give yourself a much greater chance that they will pick you because they will remember you the most.

It's been said that the average person needs to see a message an average of seven times before they will take any action on it. In today's digital age, that has increased to around thirteen times! By sending them daily emails and consistent communication, you increase the likelihood of them giving a yes response with you over the competition.

There are several types of CRMs on the market, and we will not recommend one over another. Do your homework and find one that works for you.

Remember this important Secret on Dynasty Marketing Strategy: *A fully functioning CRM system is a must.*

Secret #66

Use Social Media Smartly

Social media is a double-edged sword. It is a great way to advertise to potential customers for little or no cost, but it also can sink you if the wrong thing goes viral.

Having a knowledgeable person in charge of your social media is smart. Posting once per quarter may seem like enough, but it is not. The more engagement you have, the more the algorithm will show it to more people. They want exciting posts that get reactions from people. Reactions equal more time spent on their platform, which makes them happy.

You should post content that engages parents at least 3-4 times a week, maybe more. Look for posts that get likes and shares. These can be videos, live streams, and still photos or memes. Find what engages your followers and keep feeding them. Once in a while, slip in a classroom opening or a teacher's help wanted ad.

You want to pay for followers if you cannot get them organically. You are looking to target parents of children under five, a targeted demographic on most platforms. Do an ad to get people to like your page; these may or may not be existing customers. You want potential future customers to select your page as well. That way, you can stay front and center with them over a long period, and when they need your service, they will surely remember you.

Don't be a cheapskate and refuse to spend money on social media. To build a child care dynasty, you must think like a dynasty owner. Think big. Spending thousands of money to get followers is a good start. You may even get lucky and have one of your posts go viral, which will help you get many followers quickly.

If you have an employee that is good with social media, we recommend paying them a little extra each month and allowing them to work from home a few hours a week managing everything. We recommend seeing what your competitors are doing first, so you can make an action plan to be better than them. You will want a better website, more followers, and more engagement than they have. Doing so will make sure you are getting the most tours and enrollments!

Remember this important Secret on Dynasty Marketing Strategy: ***Use social media smartly.***

Secret #67

Reviews are Important; Don't Obsess Over Them

In today's world, reviews are essential; you just have to be careful not to obsess over them. You should have one review for every five you have in license capacity. Licensed for 100; you should have at least 20 reviews. Licensed for 50, you need to have at least 10.

Your goal is not 5.0; that is almost impossible. You should have a plan to make sure you are at 4.75 or higher. You need to get extra 5-star reviews to compensate if you have less than that. The more you get, the better shape you are in if a lousy parent tries to derail you with a 1-star review.

Experiment. Go to Google Reviews and look up your favorite restaurant. I can promise you it has 1-star reviews. It is still your favorite restaurant, isn't it? Just because one or more people have a terrible experience does not mean it is a bad place. The same thing is true about your center. Exceptionally few schools will be 5.0 schools, and it is unrealistic to have that as a goal.

The best way to get reviews is to ask kindly. If you know a parent is happy with your service, ask them if they wouldn't mind doing a review for you. Tell them you will send them a link immediately, and ask the parent if they would fill it out on the spot. Don't let them procrastinate; while they are waiting for their child to be brought to them is a perfect time.

If you have multiple centers, have a contest between directors to see who can get the most reviews in a calendar month. Directors love competition. The more reviews you get, the better, so you can dilute any negative ones that come your way.

So stop fretting if you get a 1-star review; it happens to all of us. It doesn't mean that your school is bad, and it won't be held against you as long as you can stay above 4.75 overall. Get enough 5-star reviews so that it dilutes the one stars away.

Remember this important Secret on Dynasty Marketing Strategy: ***Reviews are important; don't obsess over them.***

Secret #68

Pay Handsomely for Staff and Parent Referrals

You simply cannot rely on word-of-mouth advertising to do all of your marketing for you; it will not be enough. Having a lot of different tools in your marketing belt is the only surefire way to remain at 90% occupancy or better.

Paying for referrals may seem like a considerable expense, and it will be as long as you consider it an expense. If you look at it as an investment, it will seem much more palatable.

The lifetime value of a customer paying $250 a week in tuition and staying for three years at your school is $39,000. If you had to pay $200 or $300, or even $500 to make $39,000, would you say that was a good return on your investment?

The best referral programs we have seen are when it benefits both the referrer and the referred. Let us explain how this works.

Sally loves it at ABC Preschool. Her son Johnny has been attending for the last three years and loves his friends. Sally's friend Sara from church has a child the same age as Johnny. Sally tells Sara all about ABC Preschool and how much Johnny is learning, and Sara says she will check it out. Sally gives Sara a referral card and tells her to take it to the tour, and if she attends, they both will get a free week out of the deal.

It's a win-win for both the referred and the referral—the cost to you is $500. ($250 a week for both parties). The long-term return to you is much greater!

We recommend not giving the free week until at least the fourth week of attendance; that way, you have made a profit, and if she leaves after five weeks (unlikely), you still make money.

We recommend offering a similar deal to staff who refer staff members or children to your school, and instead of providing a free week, you give them cash. Use whatever number you think would get your employees motivated to refer someone.

Use the same policy that the money is paid after the parent has stayed four weeks; in the case of staff, I would use 60 days.

Our policy is we give a $250 bonus to new staff. $125 after 30 days and another $125 after 90 days. This works for us but may not work for you. Experiment and find a number that works for you.

Remember this important Secret on Dynasty Marketing Strategy: ***Pay handsomely for staff and parent referrals.***

Secret #69

Create Amazing Reciprocal Partnerships

If you look at big business, you will see many reciprocal partnerships formed that are mutually beneficial to both parties. American Airlines has reciprocal agreements with Alaska Airlines and also with JetBlue. Even though they are competitors, they have found a way to work together as a team to benefit both companies.

Sephora and Kohl's have formed a partnership that took Sephora's line of products and placed them in all of Kohl's locations. This is an example of a reciprocal partnership; both parties benefit from each other.

As a child care center owner, you also can go out and find reciprocal partnerships: a local hospital, a church, a school, a corporate office, or a large business. Find someone who needs child care for many people and offer that service. You are the expert; they do not know how to run child care centers.

The benefit to the business is vast; they will have priority placement in their school. They also do not have to deal with the regulatory issues associated with running a school, for which you are the expert.

This kind of partnership can be very profitable, as the business will bear the brunt of the overhead expenses. Work in a nice profit, and make sure you have a non-compete agreement with the company to keep them from kicking you out and doing it themselves after you get the center profitable. An attorney can draft the language for you.

Look around your area and see if there is a significant employer with childbearing workers. If a factory has mostly older men working at it, offering child care would not be a good idea. If the workforce has many childbearing-age females, that would be a much better investment for you. Do your homework and find a deal that works for you.

FACT: Females make over 90% of child care decisions, so this is why you would want to target them more with your marketing.

The bigger your business, the better chance you will land a sizable reciprocal partnership. Big business tends to put more trust in big business. Prove yourself in your market; eventually, they will call you looking to partner up.

Remember this important Secret on Dynasty Marketing Strategy: **Create excellent reciprocal partnerships.**

Chapter 7 Notes

Chapter 8

Building and Expanding Your Dynasty

"Everyone wants to live on top of the mountain, but all the happiness and growth occurs while you're climbing it."
~ Andy Rooney

So, you wish to build a child care dynasty. You got your mindset right, your goals and dreams are written down, you have a marketing plan, your leadership team is ready to go, and now you are prepared to expand. What do you do first?

You have done the hard part if you are a profitable single school owner. Now you just need to do it again, again, and again. Most people would think your first school is the hardest to open, but that is not the case. In our opinion, the second school is the hardest to open.

Why is the second school the hardest for most owners to open? Control. Most owners are very heavily involved in center #1. It is tough for them to let go enough to go out and open #2. Most owners feel that if they leave #1, it will fall apart without them; this is why most centers never open a second location.

We will help give you the tools to expand your business; we are experts at this. If you follow all of the Secrets in this book, you will have the tools necessary to build your child care dynasty. We can't do it for you, but we can partner with you and guide you every step of the way through our fantastic Child Care Genius University mentorship program you will learn about later in the book.

Secret #70

Carefully Evaluate Every Deal

Expansion must be done without emotion because emotion will cloud your judgment. You must look at every potential deal through an unbiased and unemotional filter.

When we look at a potential deal, Carol looks at it from a logistical standpoint. How many children can we be licensed for, how would the classrooms be set up, how many teachers would we need, how many renovations would we need, and when could we open?

Brian would evaluate the total cost of the project, how to finance it, what the profitability would be, and what the risks are. We each have our role, and if one of us were to veto the project, it does not happen. This way, neither one of us gets too emotionally involved. We have turned down projects the other one wanted and, in the long run, probably saved ourselves hundreds of thousands of dollars.

We recommend you do something similar with your business partner. Having two sets (or more) eyes on a project helps to keep things from getting missed. Always be sure that one of the people looking at the project is the financial person because the numbers have to work in the end.

If you cannot make at least 15% net profit on a location, it is probably not worth the time and effort to do the project. You will need the profit from this location to fund the down payment of location #3, so do not sell yourself short in the profit department, or you will slow your growth tremendously.

Be sure to have your CPA double-check your numbers for you and have your attorney evaluate the deal. We have advised clients to walk away from deals in the past due to red flags we have seen that you may not know even exist. We can help you evaluate a deal to ensure the numbers work for you; reach out to us at Child Care Genius University to see if our mentorship program is right for you.

Remember this important Secret on Building and Expanding Your Dynasty: ***Carefully evaluate every deal.***

Secret #71

Site Selection is Important

In the last Secret, we discussed keeping emotion out of decision-making; this also holds for site selection. Do your market research to ensure that the site you select is one parents will drive to and drop their children off.

What is the average income of the parents that live in the area within three miles of the school? What is the average family size? What are the home values? All of these things matter when it comes to school placement.

These issues are less important when buying an existing school, providing that there has not been a shift in the area's demographics. Let's say a significant employer has left the area, and there were massive job losses, you would expect many people to relocate, and if older people were to replace the younger people, less child care would be needed.

Realtors are often a good resource when looking for the demographics you need to find a good location. They usually have all of the information you would want regarding site selection.

Parents today value convenience and want a smooth drop off and pick up. Be sure that traffic delays and congestion at traditional drop-off and pickup times are minimal. If you are considering a location, drive there during drop-off and pick-up times to see what a parent would experience.

Check the sex offender registry to see who lives near the school. In some states, you will have to notify parents if there are any within a few miles; that's why it is good to know ahead of time.

Is the area quiet? Are you close to an airport where large planes will be overhead during naptime? Are train tracks nearby, and a train whistle can blow and wake children? These are all things to consider when looking for a location.

What about the crime in the neighborhood? Is there a police station nearby? Do they patrol regularly? What is the building security like? Will the parents be able to drop off and pick up without fear of criminals? Will the kids be safe when playing outside?

There is a lot to think of when choosing a new location. If this is your second location, it is even scarier. Do your homework, have patience, keep emotions out of it, and have a game plan for success. Let us know if we can help in any way. We are cheering for your success!

Remember this important Secret on Building and Expanding Your Dynasty: ***Site selection is important.***

Secret #72

Ensure That You Are Properly Insured

The bigger your business grows, the more liability you will have. The deeper your pockets develop, the more someone will want to sue you if things go wrong. Do not let that scare you; ensure your way to peace of mind.

It would help if you had a child care insurance specialist as your advocate. Why can't I use the agent who has been insuring my car and house for a long time? The answer is simple; they are not specialists in our industry.

Would you go to your family doctor for open heart surgery? Probably not. Regardless of how well you know them or how well they know you. Why? Because they are not a specialist.

You need someone that knows our industry inside and out and willing to tell you the types of insurance you need and the coverage limits you need on each policy.

You hope and pray that you never have a claim, but you will be glad you have the proper coverage when you do!

We have been using Aleaf Insurance for many years; it is the only company we recommend. We love them so much and know how important it is for you to call them that we wanted them to be the ONLY company we promote in this book.

You can reach the Aleaf Insurance Child Care Division by visiting https://www.aleafinsurance.com/child-care.

Remember this important Secret on Building and Expanding Your Dynasty: *Ensure that you are properly insured.*

Secret #73

Shared Resources Offer Huge Benefits

As your child care dynasty grows, you have the opportunity to share resources and drive the costs of running your business down. Keeping costs down increases the bottom line, which is always good.

The benefits of multiple locations are numerous. We will list some cost savings measures for growing a large business.

1. **Staff sharing:** The ability to share staff between locations is a huge advantage and a significant cost savings measure. When a single place is understaffed or overstaffed, the owner must call someone in or have someone go home, cutting hours. A multi-center owner can shift employees around to maximize staffing at all locations, and with multi-

centers, there is more of a chance that someone wants to go home early when there is overstaffing.

2. **Buying in Bulk:** The more extensive your operation, the more you can reduce the cost of supplies and food. You can buy in bulk which saves money.

3. **Centralized Tours:** Having one person responsible for tours for multiple schools allows the on-site directors to focus on staff and parents, thus lowering staff and parent turnover.

4. **Marketing Savings:** You will have one website and one social media page on each platform, thus cutting costs. You will be able to place one paid advertisement and cover several locations. The cost of your marketing is shared between the sites. Multiple locations allow your schools to be much more well-known in the community, increasing word-of-mouth advertising.

5. **Admin Cost:** The cost of your administrative team is shared among more locations, which increases the bottom line.

6. **Parent/Employee Convenience:** Opening a center across town or in another city allows parents or employees who live closer a chance to save money on commuting; plus if you have a parent or employee move, you may have a location closer to where they now live.

Remember this important Secret on Building and Expanding Your Dynasty: ***Shared resources offer huge benefits.***

Secret #74

Look for Your Competitive Edge
and Exploit it

What do you do better than your competitors? That is your most significant selling point. Do you have one? Then you need to find one and exploit it to the fullest.

Your staff is your biggest asset. How educated are they? How much experience do they have? How loving are they to the children? How long have they been with you? These are all major selling points.

Your curriculum is also a central competitive selling point. What a child will learn at school is number one on a parent's mind when they tour and attend. Be sure to pick an excellent curriculum that no one in your area uses, or create your own as we did.

We wanted a curriculum that was the best in our state, so we took the time and money to create it. It is our most vital selling point on tours and why we have such satisfied parents.

Location can be a selling point if you are convenient for many people. In our case, we have centers in all corners of our city, so no one in our area has to drive more than ten minutes to reach one of our locations. It gives us a significant competitive edge.

Find your strengths and exploit them in all of your marketing and your tours. You only have a few minutes to sell them on you; bring your best attributes.

Remember this important Secret on Building and Expanding Your Dynasty: ***Look for your competitive edge and exploit it.***

Secret #75

Have Duplicatable Systems

There is power in duplication. When you walk into a McDonald's restaurant, you can order a Big Mac from any one in the world. A franchise owner named Bob cannot call the sandwich a Big Bob. Why? Because they have a duplicatable system.

Your dynasty needs to have the same type of duplicatable systems to make expansion easier. Why reinvent the wheel each time you open a location? Build systems so employees who transfer from one location to another have the same processes, with nothing new to learn. This makes training and expansion much more accessible.

Your core process manual and your operations manual will lay out your duplicatable systems to have, be sure your staff members are familiar with them and know how to access them if they have questions.

Remember that the locations do not have to be identical, only the operating systems. The more you duplicate, the smoother the operation will run. The ultimate goal is for the business to operate independently of you, which makes it easier to exit one day. The more duplicatable it is, the more it will be worth in the long run.

Remember this important Secret on Building and Expanding Your Dynasty: *Have duplicatable systems.*

Secret #76

Consider Franchising as an Option

We have had several clients go franchising with their child care business. In almost every instance, the client built the program to 5-7 corporate-owned schools before attempting to franchise the concept.

Franchising is when an owner of a brand's trademarked business system (franchisor) allows another (franchisee) to pay an initial fee (franchise fee) and a monthly royalty (usually based on a percentage of sales) for the right to do business under the franchisor's name and system.

Franchising is expensive to start(up to $250,000 or more) but will amortize over time as franchises are sold.

Be sure to hire a franchise attorney to help you navigate the legal hurdles you would need to cross should you decide to begin franchising. Each state has its own rules and regulations to operate inside its borders.

If done correctly, franchising can be a great way to build your child care dynasty and create long-term generational wealth. If done wrong, it could bankrupt you. Be sure to be adequately capitalized before beginning the process.

Remember this important Secret on Building and Expanding Your Dynasty: **Consider franchising as an option**.

Secret #77

Timing is Everything

As a child care center owner, you must constantly be on the lookout for market trends and be willing to pivot quickly. Timing is everything.

When we were first starting out in our first child care center 25 years ago, radio advertising was big. We invested heavily, and it worked very well for us. When satellite radio came on the scene, people did not listen to local radio as much, so we quickly pivoted to online advertising, which was new at the time. Some of my competitors are still on the radio today.

Wayne Gretsky, a famous hockey player, once said, *"Skate to where the puck is going to be, not where it is."*

In all areas of your business, you need to be ahead of the times, not behind them.

If your parents or employees are not signing in electronically every morning, you are behind the times.

If you are still advertising in a newspaper, you are behind the times.

It is essential that you stay ahead of the times. Always be looking for trends in your market; this is one of the most important reasons to join a mentorship group. It can help you know what your market trends are.

When you want to expand, put a center where the kids will be in five years, not where they are now. Look for neighborhoods where parents with young children are moving in and replacing older people with no children; not the other way around!

If you have a factory in your city that is a significant employer, can that business possibly go under in the next few years, and you lose many parents? Look at the industry and the likelihood of long-term survivability. Detroit used to be a booming auto manufacturing town, but now many neighborhoods are vacant due to plant closures.

As your business grows, remember that timing is everything, and always think three moves ahead of your competition. The early bird gets the worm, but the second mouse gets the cheese. Be strategic and skate to where the puck WILL BE.

Remember this important Secret on Building and Expanding Your Dynasty: *Timing is everything.*

Secret #78

Fail Forward

The best hitters in major league baseball average .300, meaning they only get a hit 30% of the time. Imagine making millions of dollars by failing 70% of the time.

Babe Ruth was a home run king in his day, but he was also the strike-out king. Why? Because he was not afraid to fail. He was always trying to hit a home run, and because of that, he struck out a lot.

In business, you will never hit a home run 100% of the time.

We have seen owners of centers that have not made a profit in years and are trying to make it profitable to no avail. You cannot take a dead horse and drag him across the finish line; some centers just need to close.

We have closed a few schools that were not as profitable as we had hoped. Our time is so valuable that if we cannot make enough profit, it is not worth our time, and we will close the school or sell it.

We have all seen franchise restaurants close. Imagine paying millions in royalties and franchise fees only to close your restaurant. It happens all of the time. Do you know why? Because market forces change. A good business location today might not be a good location tomorrow.

Never throw good money after bad money. Do not let your performing schools subsidize your underperforming schools, give it your best effort, then either sell the school or close it. Take your time, effort, and energy into trying a different area. Eventually, you will hit some home runs.

Remember this important Secret on Building and Expanding Your Dynasty: *Fail forward.*

Secret #79

Ten Centers are Easier to Manage Than One

We never worked harder than when we had only one school. We did everything and worked seven days a week, 12 hours a day, and made very little money.

We were happy we had our own business but frustrated at how hard we had to work.

When we opened location number two, things started to change. We realized we could not be in two places at once and started delegating. With delegation, we realized we did not have to work so hard.

By the time we opened our tenth school, we were working less than ever. We had a leadership team that handled the day-to-day, and we could work when we wanted at what we wanted. We were able to pivot to the real estate investment business and build an extensive investment portfolio in a brief period.

The most challenging center to open is the second school. It requires the owner to give up control. The school they built, nurtured, and cried over has to be handed over to someone else, which is very difficult.

Many owners never open a second school because they can't figure out how to give up control of center #1. Often they work so hard on center number one that they feel they have no time to do a second school. They think it will be twice the work, but it will not be.

If you have one school and want a second one, we can help you put those systems in place to allow you to break free and delegate yourself right out of a job. Just reach out to us at info@childcaregenius.com and say HELP!

Remember this important Secret on Building and Expanding Your Dynasty: ***Ten centers are easier to manage than one.***

Chapter 8 Notes

Chapter 9

Financing Your Dynasty

"Finance is not merely about making money. It's about achieving our deep goals and protecting the fruits of our labor. It's about stewardship and, therefore, about achieving a good society."
~ Robert J. Shiller

Expansion takes money and lots of it. It may seem impossible to think about growth if you are struggling financially. It's time to change your mindset and start getting a plan to make your goals and dreams come true.

We got to four schools without ever coming out of pocket more than $10,000. We used other people's money (landlord funding) to help us open centers and grow.

We then used the money from those four locations to expand even more significantly, and we started opening more schools.

We have coached clients that bought an existing school for as low as $5,000. There are deals out there; it is time to find them. We can help you!

We teach our Child Care Genius University clients how to find centers to buy that are not even on the market! Check out chapter 11 for additional resources to help you with your expansion goals.

Secret #80

Consider a REIT (Real Estate Investment Trust)

If you are looking to finance your next child care location, one option to consider is a Real Estate Investment Trust. A REIT would purchase a property for you and also give you some working capital in exchange for a long-term lease on the property. You may or may not have a buy-out provision at the end of the lease term.

Benefits: It allows you to buy a property for little to no money down and not have to go through traditional bank qualifications. If you are in rapid expansion mode, banks may see you as a credit risk if you are overextended. A REIT is willing to take some risks banks will not.

Drawbacks: The effective interest rate you will pay on a REIT will be higher than you would get with bank financing, so it will cost you much more over your lease term. Plus, at the end of your lease term, you still do not have property ownership in most cases.

We do not take a position either way on REITs because there are instances where they can be beneficial. Our rule is to use these as an option ONLY if bank or owner financing is not an option.

Remember this important Secret on Financing Your Dynasty: *Consider a REIT (Real Estate Investment Trust).*

Secret #81

Private Equity or Venture Capital
is an Option

We have had several clients over the last few years get private equity and venture capital to rapidly expand their child care dynasty. How it works is an investor group pulls together a large sum of money and backs the expansion of certain types of businesses. Child care is becoming a very popular area for this type of financing due to its monthly recurring revenue model.

Similar to REIT, the interest rate you normally pay with this type of financing will normally be higher than a bank, but banks would be much more cautious about rapid expansion. With the increased risk comes increased costs which will be passed down to you.

If you are looking for rapid expansion and have an investor group willing to front you building costs and working capital, it is not a bad way to rapidly build a child care dynasty.

This financing is normally only offered to successful child care businesses with multiple locations and proven profitability. This way, the risk is reduced.

Remember this important Secret on Financing Your Dynasty: ***Private equity or venture capital is an option.***

Secret #82

Bankroll Your Expansion with Personal Savings

We do not like debt and built our entire child care operation for the first 17 years without borrowing from a bank. We bought three competitors and paid them cash to purchase their businesses.

While this sounds appealing to most people, we wish we would have done it differently. At the end of 17 years, we did not own any of our child care buildings.

We spent the next eight years buying all of our buildings except one, and every one was bought through owner financing.

If you can buy a center with cash, it is great to not have to borrow it. You can save interest, plus you get to save available borrowing credit for building purchases in the future.

Remember that before you use your cash, make sure you have enough savings for emergencies and recessions.

Debt is not a bad thing if you use it wisely. It took us a while to figure that out; the secret is to keep your debt-to-income ratio as low as possible.

Remember this important Secret on Financing Your Dynasty: ***Bankroll your expansion with personal savings.***

Secret #83

Use Other People's Money When Available

We have owner financed almost $5 million worth of properties over the last 25 years with four different people. You can say we are pretty good at using other people's money.

Our net worth was $4 million before we stepped into a bank and asked for a loan to buy a piece of property. You can say that that bank was very happy to meet us at that point.

It all started a year after we went bankrupt in 1995 after a failed business. We were living in a rented house, and we took a walk one day, and a guy was putting up a sign, FOR SALE BY OWNER, $119,900, 12 acres with a 3BR house.

Deciding to be bold and honest, we asked the guy if he would consider owner financing (since we would never qualify for a loan), and he said he would consider it. We struck a deal and agreed to pay him $1022 monthly for 20 years (8% interest). We also agreed that we would not pay off the note early since this was his retirement.

We made every one of those 240 payments and paid that house off. We could have refinanced it but never did because we gave this man our word we would not. He took a chance on us, and we were not going to let him down. Our word is our bond.

Since then, we have met other people in our life who have financed properties for us and mentored us in the field of real estate. We helped these owners avoid some taxes through owner financing, and they helped us to avoid some of the fees and expenses of bank financing. It was a win-win.

Do not be afraid to ask about owner financing, especially when interest rates start climbing. An owner who owns a building free and clear may want to delay some of the capital gains and can do so through owner financing.

We could get the financing due to the relationships we created as tenants. Not one of them ran a credit check on us or asked us for a financial statement. In each case, we began by renting a space and being amazing tenants. Over time we convinced the landlord that selling to us was the best long-term option for them.

Seller financing is a great way for property owners to spread the capital gains from their property over time, which may help them later in life.

Seller financing seldom shows up on a credit check, and normally the interest rate is very close to current bank rates. We never paid more than a 5% down payment on any of the seven properties we have owner financed. Our bank wanted a 25% down payment.

Besides our house, we paid off every one of our owner-financed properties in five years with an aggressive pay-down policy. We wanted our properties mortgage free as soon as possible so we can use them to leverage bank financing for more expensive properties, as described in Secret #86.

If you are looking for guidance on how to ask your landlord if they will owner finance your property, feel free to reach out to us at info@childcaregenius.com, we are happy to help.

Remember this important Secret on Financing Your Dynasty: **Use other people's money when available.**

Secret #84

SBA Loans are a Low Down

Payment Option

Using the Small Business Administration (SBA) is an option to purchase an existing school or a child care building.

The SBA will guarantee the loan with an SBA-authorized lender (normally your local bank). If you default, the SBA will pay off any losses to your lender, making them whole. The risk is solely on the SBA.

Normally with these types of loans, you have to have a solid business plan and a 10% down payment. You can finance the property, equipment, and working capital.

Many of our former clients have used SBA financing, and we highly recommend this option. There are a lot of hurdles to jump through for approval, and it is a lengthy approval process, but normally the interest rate is very good, and the loan terms are generous.

 this important Secret on Financing Your Dynasty: **SBA loans are a low down payment option.**

Secret #85

Use Relationships for Traditional Bank Financing

We belong to the largest credit union in our state. We chose them over 25 years ago because they were convenient, and they had a large portfolio of financing options that I would eventually need access to.

We built relationships at our credit union with bank managers, loan officers, the president, the COO, and the tellers. We were loved and appreciated by them because we took the time to get to know them. We became one of their largest customers over time.

We met with the commercial loan supervisor five years before we ever needed to borrow funds and made sure we knew exactly what she would be looking for from us when we needed to borrow.

When it was time to start borrowing millions of dollars for our phase 2 expansion, we leaned on all of our relationships and were able to get things done in record time. Have you ever heard of the phrase it's not what you know but who you know? Well, it's true. We were able to buy properties and close in 4-6 weeks, which is attractive to a seller of a property when entertaining offers.

Start now at building those relationships you will need later. If you wait until you need them, you will have a transactional relationship. If you build the relationship first, you will get a whole different level of service.

This relationship won't get you approved if you have bad credit; they cannot change the federal guidance they must follow. What the relationships will allow you to do is have the benefit of the doubt when it is a close call. When your appraisal is late, you will have them make a call and lean on them to speed it up. When the underwriter calls for clarification, the loan officer goes to bat for you. Relationships are key to building a child care dynasty!

Remember this important Secret on Financing Your Dynasty: *Use relationships for traditional bank financing.*

Secret #86

Use Real Estate to Leverage
More Real Estate

Wealth can create more wealth if done correctly. What we mean by this is that when you own a property free and clear without a mortgage, the power of that property is huge when it comes to leveraging other property.

We have begun using this method to finance the down payments on the new property we are purchasing. We can buy millions in properties with no money down, which is a great way to conserve cash.

Let's say you own a property worth $250,000 that is mortgage free. Most banks can use that property's equity as your down payment without having to refinance the original property.

In the above example, my credit union will multiply $250k by 75%, which equals $187,500. That $187,500 can now be used to secure a property worth $750,000. In this example, you can buy a $750,000 piece of property for no money down just by offering up the mortgage-free property as collateral.

The credit union will place a second mortgage on the property, but you will not owe any money on the original property. As long as you pay your note as agreed on the new property, you have nothing to worry about. Default on your new property, and they can take both of your properties (as the old one is your collateral). Remember, these are assets that can be sold if you ever got into financial trouble, and then you can simply pay off the mortgage.

This is why we have an aggressive pay down plan on our real estate mortgages. We know that in five years, when we pay off a building, it becomes a future down payment to buy a property worth three times the value, and then the process starts again. How about that for creating generational wealth?

Remember this important Secret on Financing Your Dynasty: *Use real estate to leverage more real estate.*

Secret #87

Sometimes Leasing is Better
Than Owning

Owning is not always the best option for building your child care dynasty. Leasing sometimes is the best option, and we want you to always be open-minded on every deal to decide the best way to proceed.

Leasing is the best option in the following situations:

1. When the cost of real estate has skyrocketed, it is much cheaper to rent, at least initially.
2. When interest rates are higher than 8% (unless you can pay it off in five years and save a lot of interest).
3. When the market may be unstable due to job losses or an economic downturn.
4. When you have bad credit and cannot get financing.

As we said, we leased all our centers for the first 17 years; we did not know any better. We still lease one of our buildings because the lease is very attractive and much cheaper than owning.

If you decide to lease, be a great tenant and build a great relationship with your landlord. Fix little things yourself, do not bug your landlord with petty things. Doing so will build faith that you can leverage in the future.

Maybe this person will buy another building for you to lease or eventually sell to you with owner financing. If you complain when the rent is raised and call for every little issue, a sweet deal will probably never come. Be the kind of tenant you would like to have if you owned the place.

Remember this important Secret on Financing Your Dynasty: *Sometimes leasing is better than owning.*

Secret #88

Use Caution When Borrowing From a Friend or Relative

This is one way of financing that we would not recommend because we have seen it go badly more times than not.

If you are going to borrow from a friend or relative, we recommend you do not give any equity in the business but instead do a legal document with you borrowing the money from them at a set interest rate for a set number of months. In our opinion, this works the best.

When these people get fractional ownership interest, feelings can get hurt if they do not think you are getting them a decent return fast enough. They might want to help you run the business to speed things up, causing many issues. We have seen it numerous times, be careful!

Remember this important Secret on Financing Your Dynasty: ***Use caution when borrowing from a friend or relative.***

Chapter 9 Notes

_____
_____
_____
_____
_____
_____
_____
_____
_____

Chapter 10

Exit Strategy

"Every exit is an entry somewhere else."
~ Tom Stoppard

Some day in the future, you will want to retire, and preparing early for that day will allow you to get the best possible return on your investment. We have seen owners work their whole lives 60+ hours a week for 30 years+ and in the end, have nothing to show for it financially.

We are here to help. These next six Secrets will help you with some tools for success. If you fail to plan, then you are planning to fail.

In Chapter 11, there are additional resources to help your business with a long-term exit strategy plan. We are here to help you grow, succeed, and retire with financial freedom.

Secret #89

Know When it is the Right Time to Sell

Trying to teach you when the right time to sell your child care business is aking to us trying to tell you when to sell your stocks. The proper answer to both is when you need to and at the highest possible price.

We are hoping you are not ready to throw in the towel quite yet. We know many of you had a tough time during the 2020-2021 pandemic and the 2022 hiring crisis, but if you survived that, you will be able to survive anything!

As part of your selling decision, include a 1-2 year build-up plan before selling. We mean that you work with us and let us help you get your center working at peak performance, which will help improve the value.

You would not sell your house without painting it and fixing anything broken, would you? Because you know a few dollars invested will be returned to you manyfold.

The same concept applies. Your business needs to be operating at peak performance, your center needs to be 95%+ full, your employees need to be able to work independently, and you, as the owner, need to work outside the center at least 80% of the time. At that point, you can get top dollar for your school.

We help center owners prepare to sell by getting their systems in peak working order, increasing profitability, full enrollment, happy employees, and having an owner working from home.

Reach out to us if you want us to get your business ready to sell in 1-2 years, and we will work with you and develop an amazing plan to get you there. For others with a 10-20 year sales plan, we can help you get there too. Reach out to info@childcaregenius.com.

Remember this important Secret on Exit Strategy: ***Know when it is the right time to sell.***

Secret #90

Sales Value Increases as the

Dynasty Expands

When it is time to sell, you want to get the most money possible. The more locations in your dynasty, the better the sale price you will get for your company.

Someone with ten centers will be able to sell for much more (per location) than someone with only one. That is because of the power of the dynasty. Future owners will pay a premium to add a big group of centers into their portfolios. We have seen the value of multiple schools to be more than three times that of a single school.

Factor this into your long-term exit strategy to maximize the value of your schools. Keeping in mind that you will have to pay a large capital gain on the sale, the more you can make, the better the net return on your investment.

Remember this important Secret on Exit Strategy: ***Sales value increases as the dynasty expands.***

Secret #91

Selling to an Employee or Family Member is an Option

If you have an executive director or an onsite director that has been with you a very long time and knows your operation inside and out, consider selling to this person. You may also want to turn over your operation to the next generation and let your child or children run the school. We have seen both of these options done very successfully.

If this is a possibility, take 2-3 years and slowly train them in all areas of business ownership. In the case of selling to a non-relative, be sure to get them to sign a confidentiality agreement before giving them any insider information. If they change their mind, you are protected from them divulging insider information.

In the case of a child or children you want to sell to, be sure to have the child work at the school from an early age. Make sure this child does every job at the school and works their way up the ladder. Be sure to pay your child the same wage as everyone else and show NO favoritism whatsoever.

If you want your child to someday be in leadership and get respect, it will never happen if they have not earned it. All of our children have worked at our school, and not once have they ever gotten any special treatment. Our executive director has rejected their time off requests many times, and we never intervene.

When they graduated college and took on leadership roles, they were respected by everyone on our staff because they earned their way to the top. You may think you are doing your child a favor by putting your finger on the scale, but we can promise you that is not the case.

Keep in mind that if you sell to a family member or employee, more than likely, you will need to owner finance most, if not all, of the cost. Remember that this is not a bad thing from a tax perspective.

Be sure to do everything through an attorney and have a clause that you can come in and take it back over should the business turn unprofitable and they cannot make their payments to you; that way, you are protected.

Remember this important Secret on Exit Strategy: ***Selling to an employee or family member is an option.***

Secret #92

Be Sure to Pick the Right Real Estate Broker

When you are ready to sell, be sure to find a real estate broker that you can trust, one that specializes in child care business sales. Do not call your uncle who is in real estate and ask him to list it (unless your uncle is a child care center sales specialist).

The main reason you want a child care sales specialist is they will have access to hundreds of potential buyers, some of whom may be out of your country. Your local agent does not have these types of contacts.

Establish a relationship with a child care real estate broker 2-3 years before you plan on selling, that way, you can get help from them on increasing the value before it is time to sell.

Remember this important Secret on Exit Strategy: ***Be sure to pick the right real estate broker.***

Secret #93

Do Proper Estate Planning

Years before you plan on selling, be sure to sit down with an estate planning attorney and a tax attorney to fully understand the implications of selling your business.

If you have substantial wealth from the sale, you will want to make sure you minimize taxes and protect your estate for your heirs in case of your passing.

We have seen many owners use trusts to be able to pass on wealth to heirs without having a lengthy probate process. If you have a net worth of over $1 million, now is the time for estate planning to ensure you and your family are protected.

Remember this important Secret on Exit Strategy: ***Do proper estate planning.***

Secret #94

Use Real Estate to Build
Generational Wealth

Once we started buying property, we got an adrenaline rush and wanted more. We got excited each time we added a new property to our portfolio. We initially used the profits from our child care business to fund the down payments on rental properties.

Real estate is an amazing part of a good exit strategy. Owning your own school building is the first part; owning multi-family rental units is an amazing wealth creator as well. The rentals that you buy will significantly reduce your child care income tax burden, and they will produce passive income each and every month.

Our system is complicated, but we will give you the basics here.

1. Buy a multi-family (2-4 units) apartment building using a 25% down payment from profits from your child care center.
2. Use the rent the tenants pay to pay your mortgage and maintenance.
3. Depreciate the asset and reduce your taxes
4. Your tenants are now building your wealth.
5. Repeat, over and over.

The hardest part is knowing how to find the right property, which is where we come in. We teach our proven wealth creation system inside the upper levels of our *Child Care Genius University* coaching and training program. We teach you the following:

1. How to know what a good return on investment is for multi-family apartments.
2. How to calculate your profit.
3. How to structure your real estate business for tax purposes
4. How to buy properties with no money down
5. How to create an eight-figure net worth in the next 10-15 years

Owning your school buildings and multi-family apartments is an excellent way to retire with amazing generational wealth. When you sell your schools, keep the real estate! Your asset will pay you a top-dollar passive income until you die, worth even more to the next generation.

For more information on *Child Care Genius University*, visit ChildCareGenius.com/University.

Remember this important Secret on Exit Strategy: ***Use real estate to build generational wealth.***

Chapter 10 Notes

_____
_____
_____
_____
_____
_____
_____
_____
_____
_____
_____
_____
_____
_____
_____
_____
_____
_____
_____
_____
_____
_____
_____
_____
_____
_____
_____
_____

Chapter 11

Additional Resources

"Your greatest asset is your earning ability. Your greatest resource is your time."
~ Brian Tracy

If you are still reading, we applaud you for trying to digest as much information as possible. If you want even more information after you finish this book, refer to the resources in the next seven Secrets. We guarantee that they will change your life and your business forever.

If we can ever help you in your business, please contact us at info@childcaregenius.com.

Secret #95

Join the Child Care Genius Mastermind™ Group

We run a FREE Facebook Mastermind Group called the Child Care Genius Mastermind. It is a great free resource for owners of programs large and small. It is a chance to network with other owners to help you solve a problem.

If you are feeling alone and want to join a group of owners for a free support system, visit Facebook.com/groups/childcaregenius and request to join. We allow current and future owners, large and small.

Remember this important Secret: ***Join the Child Care Genius Mastermind Group*™.**

Secret #96

Enroll in Child Care Genius University™

We have developed one of the most advanced child care coaching, training, and mentorship platforms in the world, and we want you to consider enrolling in *Child Care Genius University.*

We are the only large-scale child care coaching program worldwide that does one-on-one coaching and training as part of enrollment. You will have a coach that works with you regularly to help you increase profits, lower staff turnover, convert more tours to enrollments, expand, and give you peace of mind knowing you are not alone as a child care owner.

If you are struggling with any area of your business, check us out today. We have the tools to help you succeed, and results are GUARANTEED!

Enrollment is limited to keep class sizes small, so check us out today at ChildCareGenius.com/University. You will be glad that you did!

Remember this important Secret: ***Enroll in Child Care Genius University*™.**

Secret #97

Read Child Care Mindset: 30 Days of Growth and Transformation™

Mindset is so important to the business builder, but it is often the area most overlooked. Many owners are so busy getting through their day that they never take the time to look inside and develop the person staring at them in the mirror.

You are the leader of your child care dynasty; you are the boss. Many people count on you to be the best version of yourself each and every day. Do not let people down; work on yourself by reading the ***Child Care Mindset: 30 Days of Growth and Transformation*** book.

We wrote this book to help you grow as a person and leader. We will help you manage stress better and be a better spouse, a better parent, and a better person. We all have issues; let us help you with yours.

Visit ChildCareGenius.com/books and order a copy today. You will be glad you did! It is truly life-changing. Once you have worked on you, then you can order a copy for all of your team members. We know many of them need help as well.

If you would like to order more than 50 copies, we can give you special pricing; send us an email at info@childcaregenius.com.

Remember this important Secret: ***Read Child Care Mindset: 30 Days of Growth and Transformation™.***

Secret #98

Use the Child Care Mindset: Dreams, Goals, and Gratitude Journal™ Daily

The best tool we have ever created has to be our ***Child Care Mindset: Dreams, Goals, and Gratitude Journal***. It has the most impact on those that have purchased it and use it every day.

In this journal, we teach you how to have a vision and a spirit of thankfulness. In the first part, we teach you how to write your long-term dreams down and then show you how to set goals to accomplish those dreams.

Those that write down their goals and dreams are 100 times more likely to achieve them!

We also give you a place to write down things you are grateful for daily. Doing so helps keep you grounded. We give you a place to write over 1,000 things you are grateful for. The next time you are upset and feeling sad, open up your journal to the gratitude section and start reading. You will quickly change your mindset.

This is one of the most important things you can do for success. Order your copy at ChildCareGenius.com/Books. If you want special pricing on more than 50 copies (for your team), send an email to info@childcaregenius.com.

Remember this important Secret: ***Use the Child Care Mindset: Dreams, Goals, and Gratitude Journal™ Daily.***

Secret #99

Attend a Child Care Genius Conference

Twice a year, we host a live conference for child care owners and leaders around the world.

Imagine attending a conference where you learn how to take your child care business to the next level. There will be experts teaching topics such as reducing staff turnover, expansion, diversification, exit strategy, team synergy, leadership, profitability, finances, marketing, and much more.

Visit ChildCareGenius.com for more information or to get tickets.

Remember this important Secret: ***Attend a Child Care Genius Conference.***

Secret #100

Attend a Child Care Genius Workation

Work hard, play harder is a motto we like to live our life by. We have vacationed in the Caribbean 4-5 times a year for the last 15 years, and we consider it our happy place.

Once in the pool, we started talking about how great it would be to bring child care business owners with us and coach them during the week. We both would be able to write the trip off on our taxes, and we would all have a fun, relaxing week!

In 2022 we hosted our first *Child Care Genius Workation*, which was a huge success. We took four couples to Sandals Grande St. Lucian on the beautiful island of St. Lucia.

We spent no more than three hours a day doing coaching, then the rest of the day, we all hung out by the pool or the beach. We made lifelong friends and had an absolute blast.

Each couple told us it was the best money they could have invested in their business and in their relationship. We tackle topics that no one else does; that makes us different.

We plan on doing 3-4 trips a year; we would love to have you join us! Visit ChildCareGenius.com/Workation for more information.

You deserve a tax-deductible vacation!

Remember this important Secret: **Attend a Child Care Genius Workation.**

Secret #101

Book a Coaching Call with One of
Our Child Care Coaches

You can probably notice we love to help child care owners large and small! It is a passion of ours we have had for many years. We have written six books, do a weekly podcast, write a weekly blog, speak at conferences, and still run our own schools!

It is our mission to change the world, one center owner at a time. If you are struggling in any area of your business and need help, we want to help you!

We have a team of coaches (we call them professors) who are here to help grow your business. Brian does most of these calls himself, but on occasion, he gets help from one of his team members.

We guarantee that you will walk away from each call with 2-3 action items you can implement right away in your program! What are you waiting for, let's book a call today!

Each business is limited to one free call annually. This call is for current and future child care center owners and in-home family child care providers. *Students of Child Care Genius University are not eligible for this free call (they have a coach).*

Just visit https://childcaregenius.com/coaching/ to schedule your call today.

Remember this important Secret: ***Book a coaching call with one of our child care coaches.***

Chapter 11 Notes

Printed in Great Britain
by Amazon

27285267R00096